Gravity, Steam, and Steel

An Illustrated History of Rogers Pass on the Canadian Pacific Railway

Graeme Pole

I find that the snow-slides on the Selkirks are much more serious than I anticipated, and I think are quite beyond your ideas of their magnitude and of the danger to the line.

JAMES ROSS, CPR WESTERN CONSTRUCTION SUPERINTENDENT,
IN A LETTER TO WILLIAM CORNELIUS VAN HORNE,
CPR VICE-PRESIDENT, FEBRUARY 19, 1885.

Above: A Pacific Express waits on the main line at Glacier Station west of Rogers Pass, in the glory days of steam, ca. 1910.

FIFTH
HOUSE

Cover and interior design by John Luckhurst
Maps: Scott Manktelow Design
Front cover illustration: *Canadian Pacific Railway* (1985) © 2008 Tucker Smith, Courtesy of the Greenwich Workshop, Inc.
Edited and copy edited by Kirsten Craven

The publisher gratefully acknowledges the support of The Canada Council for the Arts and the Department of Canadian Heritage.

 Canada Council Conseil des Arts
for the Arts du Canada

We acknowledge the financial support of the Government of Canada through the Book Publishing Industry Development Program (BPIDP) for our publishing activities.

Printed in Canada on Forest Stewardship Council (FSC) Approved paper

ANCIENT FOREST™ FRIENDLY

Preserving our environment
Fitzhenry & Whiteside chose to print the pages of this book on recycled paper and saved these resources[1]:

energy	water	greenhouse gases	solid waste
12 million BTUs	26,603 L	685 kg	364 kg

Printed by **Webcom Inc.** on Legacy Offset 100% post-consumer waste.

trees were saved for our forests

FSC

Mixed Sources
Product group from well-managed forests, controlled sources and recycled wood or fiber

Cert no. SW-COC-002358
www.fsc.org
© 1996 Forest Stewardship Council

[1]Estimates were made using the Environmental Defense Paper Calculator.

2009 / 1

First published in the United States in 2009 by
Fitzhenry & Whiteside
311 Washington Street
Brighton, Massachusetts, 02135

Library and Archives Canada Cataloguing in Publication
Pole, Graeme, 1956-
Gravity, steam, and steel : an illustrated history of Rogers Pass on the Canadian Pacific Railway / Graeme Pole.
Includes bibliographical reference and index.
ISBN 978-1-897252-46-8
1. Railroads—British Columbia—Rogers Pass—Design and construction—History.
2. Canadian Pacific Railway Company—History. 3. Rogers Pass (B.C.)—History. I. Title.
HE2810.C2P64 2009   385.09711'68   C2009-901486-6

Fifth House Ltd.   1-800-387-9776
A Fitzhenry & Whiteside Company   www.fitzhenry.ca

Contents

Above: The third Rogers Pass station in the early 1900s.

Acknowledgements

I acknowledge a special debt to the many photographers of the historical era whose work appears in this book. Although some wined and dined with free passage in company railway cars, most eked out a living packing their cumbersome gear along a steel ribbon in the wilds to take "postcard views." Many archivists and librarians assisted with my photographic research. I am grateful to Jill Delaney and the staff at the Library and Archives Canada, Ottawa; Carol Haber and Jeannie Hounslow at the City of Vancouver Archives; Bob Kennell at the Canadian Pacific Railway Archives, Montreal; Jim Bowman and Susan Kooyman at the Glenbow Museum Archives, Calgary; Elizabeth Kundert-Cameron and Lena Goon at the Whyte Museum, Banff; Cathy English at the Revelstoke Museum Archives; and Roberto Rodriguez and Barb Eby at the Revelstoke Railway Museum. With keen eyes peeled for bent spikes and an uneven rail bed, Dave Cottingham and Marnie Pole read the first draft. Jonathan Hanna, a corporate historian emeritus for Canadian Pacific Railway, reviewed the final draft. Any derailments of fact that remain in the text are my responsibility.

Author's Notes

Chartered on February 16, 1881, the Canadian Pacific Railway Company was popularly known as "the CPR" for most of its first century of existence. Between 1968 and 1990, the railway was officially called CP Rail. In 1990, its corporate name was briefly changed to CP Rail System. In 1996, the corporation reverted to its original designation as Canadian Pacific Railway. Train buffs now call it "CP" or "Canadian Pacific." I have retained era-specific nomenclature in the text.

I refer to rail workers as men because I have found no reference to the CPR employing women in its construction ranks and train crews during the historical period described in the text.

The crest of Rogers Pass is oriented roughly north-south, whereas the general notion of the CPR is that it runs east-west. When referring to railway operations in the vicinity of Rogers Pass, the descriptions in the text, "east" and "west," should not always be interpreted literally but as pertaining to the directions of railway operations.

When computing grades on the pre-1916 track, I used the elevations from the original survey of the railway. These differ slightly from accepted elevations today. For example, in 1884, the crest of the railway grade in Rogers Pass was determined to be 4,361 feet; the elevation of the pass itself was measured at 4,351 feet. The generally accepted elevation of the watershed point in the pass today is 4,363 feet.

Although Canada began converting to metric measurements in the early 1970s, its railways continue to have mile boards, and to weigh their locomotives in tons and their rails in pounds per yard. A book about railways necessarily includes a great many numbers—dates, distances, speeds, quantities, and weights—so I have elected to use imperial measurement throughout the book for railway details to ensure integrity and accuracy, and to minimize cluttering with conversions. Metric values are given for other modern-day measurements.

1
A Needle
in a Haystack

In accounts of exploration of western Canada, the Columbia Mountains of south-central British Columbia have always played second sister to the Rocky Mountains. It is not because the Columbias are lesser mountains; it is for precisely the opposite reason. The Columbia Mountains are formidable—glacier clad, rising with sharp gradients from deeply incised valleys whose flanks are scoured by avalanche paths and cloaked by the only inland temperate rain forest in the world.

The Selkirk Range of the Columbia Mountains was a particularly hard sell to early tourists. The Rockies could boast sunrise strolls on the shores of Lake Louise, and motor launches on the Bow River. The Selkirks offered avalanche deposits taller than buildings, and tangles of alder barbed with devil's club. Their valleys were an arrangement of thickets that discouraged exploration. Consequently, the Selkirks long retained an air of mystery and remained largely unknown to all but surveyors and ardent mountaineers. Yet, these mountains played a pivotal role in Canadian history, being the final barrier to the survey and construction of the Canadian Pacific Railway (CPR)—the ribbon of steel that stitched the promise of a country together.

It was the quest for a railway route that led surveyors, location engineers, and finally, construction crews to a needle in the haystack of wild valleys in the Selkirks—a remote height of land known today as Rogers Pass. Ultimately,

the CPR laid track across the pass not because it wanted to, but because the company was running out of money and time and had no other reasonable option. In doing so, it committed to a costly and brutal battle with rock, snow, and gravity that endures more than a century later.

Chiselled to a striking profile by ice-age glaciers, the lofty spire of Mount Sir Donald (3,297 m) typifies the Selkirk Mountains.

This 1904 view to the south from the summit of Mount Sir Donald suggests the obvious: the Selkirk Mountains were a preposterous place for the CPR to consider building a railway.

2
This is the Pass for the Overland Railway

The story of how railway steel came to Rogers Pass began more than twenty years before the construction of Canada's first transcontinental railway. It centred on Walter J. Moberly, a single-minded surveyor whose contribution, unfortunately, has become a footnote to history. Moberly's surveying career began in 1852, when the twenty-year-old was hired on as an assistant construction engineer for the Ontario, Simcoe, and Huron Railway. His boss was Sandford Fleming, later engineer-in-chief of the Pacific Railway.

In 1854, Moberly purchased timber leases along the north shores of Lake Huron and Lake Superior—areas accessible only by boat. The following year he left his railway job. For three summers he explored the rugged Shield country of north-central Ontario, cutting his teeth for later travel in the wilds of BC. In the off-seasons he pursued politicians, to whom he pitched his dream: to plot the line for a railroad from Barrie, Ontario, to the Red River Settlement in what is now Manitoba.

His scheme did not find political favour, so in 1858, Moberly quit one dream for another, departing from the east for the colony of Vancouver Island and British Columbia. Moberly brashly assumed the colony's governor, James Douglas, would commission him to survey the route for a railway link to eastern Canada. It was a bold plan that eventually bore fruit, but not in a manner that Moberly could possibly have foreseen. For seven

Robbed of his place in history by pride and by circumstance, Walter Moberly became a bitter man in his later years.

frustrating years, which included a stint in jail, Moberly alternated between private exploration, politics, and employment as a surveyor with the colony of BC—never able to fully dedicate himself to his dream.

In 1865, the colonial government finally assigned Moberly to plot a road and railway route through the area drained by the Columbia River. While on his way to Seymour City on the north arm of Shuswap Lake, Moberly detoured close to the site of present-day Sicamous. At the mouth of a river that entered the lake from the east, he disturbed a pair of bald eagles by attempting to shoot the nest out from under them. The birds took flight, following the river eastward from the lake. According to his later version of events, Moberly mused that if he could follow the eagles, he might find a pass across the Gold Range (today's Monashee Mountains). If such a pass linked with the Columbia River, Moberly would have fitted a key piece into the puzzle of a railway route across BC.

Later that summer, Moberly found himself on the west bank of the Columbia River at Big Eddy, opposite the site of present-day Revelstoke. To discover if he might have been due east of the valley up which the eagles had flown, he directed his party to climb a peak on the west side of the Columbia Valley. The ascent took two days. From the summit, Moberly looked west to Shuswap Lake. The valley into which the eagles had flown wound toward him to end in a pass at the foot of his peak. From a lake in the pass, a river flowed east into the Columbia River near Big Eddy. The gradients were relatively gentle; the distance was short, and the elevation of the pass (later measured at 1,841 feet) was low. Moberly had discovered the chink in the armour of the Monashee Mountains. Unable to restrain himself, he plunged down avalanche paths from the summit to the pass, where—mimicking records left at other places by Alexander Mackenzie and David Thompson, earlier explorers of the Canadian west—he carved his name and a legend into a tree: "This is the Pass for the Overland Railway."

It was but one of the necessary passes—the railway also had to cross the Rockies and the Selkirks. Later in the season, Moberly attempted to resolve the issue of a pass across the Selkirks by exploring east from Big Eddy along the Illecillewaet River. Where the river forked, near the present-day western boundary of Glacier National Park, Moberly followed the northerly stream—now called the Tangier River—to a dead end. Winter came early and Moberly could not entice his men, who had been dining on dried squirrel meat, to travel farther. In his journal, Moberly characterized the southeast fork of the river as "the one that, judging from its general bearing, would be most likely to afford a pass in the direction wished for."

He was right in that assessment but would never personally benefit from it. The following year, Moberly sent Albert Perry to explore the pass at the head of the southeasterly fork. Although fellow surveyors called Perry "the Mountaineer," he met his match in the terrible tangle of undergrowth and on the silt-covered boulders along the Illecillewaet River. Moberly complained in his journal, "his [Perry's] failure is a great disappointment to me." The Governor of BC added to Moberly's lament by cancelling any further exploration. Moberly quit BC in late 1866 for the western US.

When BC and Canada came to terms regarding the colony's entry into Confederation in 1871, Prime Minister John A. Macdonald summoned Moberly to Ottawa to report on the best route for a railway in the new province. Moberly championed Burrard Inlet (now Vancouver) as the western terminus. From there, he stated the line should head east through the Fraser Canyon to the Thompson River, and use Eagle Pass to cross the Monashee Mountains to the Columbia River, which it should follow around the Big Bend to the Blaeberry River, crossing the Rockies at Howse Pass. Macdonald and Sandford Fleming endorsed the plan and sent Moberly west to plot the route.

Because they had to wait for BC's official entry into Confederation on July 20, it was well into summer when the teams of what was called the Pacific Survey set out from Victoria in 1871. Moberly made for Howse Pass, which he crossed with relative ease. He was so confident of the Howse Pass route—and that his superior, Sandford Fleming, would be in agreement— that he did not travel to Ottawa that winter to make a direct report. Rather than awaiting instructions for the 1872 season, he wrote his own work order, purchased a mountain of supplies on the government's tab, and prepared to make a detailed location survey of Howse Pass.

On the night before Moberly was set to depart from Victoria in April 1872, the Lieutenant-Governor of BC summoned him and handed over a telegram from Fleming. The boss decreed that Yellowhead Pass would be the route for the railway through the Rockies. Moberly was to abandon the Howse Pass survey. After racing around the colony to try to rescue unneeded supplies, a stunned Moberly complied with Fleming's order, but he had lost heart. At the end of the 1872 surveying season, Fleming fired Moberly, outraged by his excessive purchases and mediocre results. "This was joyful news for me," Moberly wrote in 1909 in his memoir, "for I saw the way clear to get out of the distasteful occupation of making useless surveys."

Moberly grew ever more bitter. His memoir contradicted information included in his own reports written four decades earlier. He claimed that Albert Perry had reached Rogers Pass at the head of the Illecillewaet River in 1866, and thus to Perry—and by implication, to Moberly—should have gone the credit for determining the line of Canada's first transcontinental railway through the Selkirk Mountains. Echoes of this ill-founded self-promotion

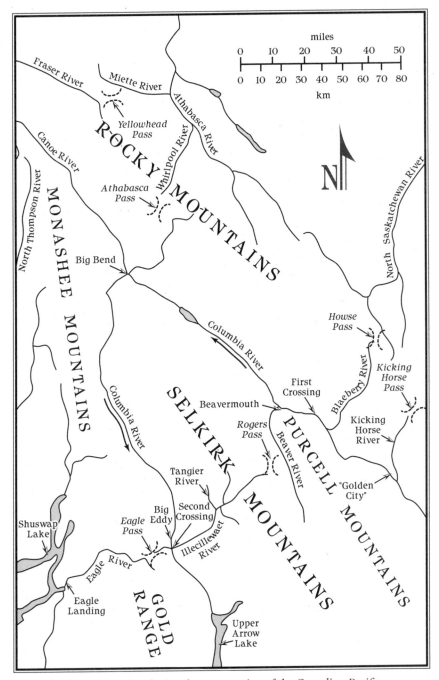

The Columbia Mountains during the construction of the Canadian Pacific Railway, 1881–1885.

continued more than seventy years later, when the writer of a history of Glacier House credited Moberly with the discovery of Rogers Pass.

Moberly need not have fabricated anything. He had roughed out a railway route from Pacific tidewater, through the valleys and canyons of the Fraser and Thompson rivers, across the Monashee Mountains to the foot of the Selkirk Mountains at the site of present-day Revelstoke. It was only 264 railway miles from there to easy ground on the prairies at Fort Calgary, but it would be twelve years before an army of surveyors and engineers, delayed by the eternal bickering of politicians, nailed down the route with ties and steel.

☆ Triple Trouble ☆

The Columbia Mountains contain four ranges. From east to west these are the Purcell Mountains, the Selkirk Mountains, the Monashee Mountains (also called the Gold Range), and, farther north, the Cariboo Mountains. By following the courses of the Columbia and Beaver rivers, the Canadian Pacific Railway looped with comparative ease around the north end of the Purcell Mountains. From the west, the railway line crossed the Monashee Mountains from Shuswap Lake, to the Columbia River by Eagle Pass. Between, the railway tackled its loftiest and most troublesome point in the Columbia Mountains head-on: the crossing of Rogers Pass in the southern Selkirks.

3
A Major Undertaking

Between 1871 and 1881, three successive federal governments toyed with the construction of Canada's first transcontinental railway. With the incorporation of the Canadian Pacific Railway Company in February 1881, Prime Minister John A. Macdonald gave the project to private enterprise. The CPR was free to choose some of the route but in other places it was constrained by track already laid by government contractors. In BC, crews led by a US contractor, Andrew Onderdonk, were building the line predominantly from west to east along the Fraser and Thompson rivers to end at Savona's Landing, just west of Fort Kamloops. In Manitoba and northwestern Ontario, contractors were laying track to link Port Arthur (now Thunder Bay) with Winnipeg.

The federal government's decision to lay track from the west toward Fort Kamloops, along with concerns about US expansion into Canadian territory in the west, factored against using Yellowhead Pass (which was too far north) to cross the Rockies. Eagle Pass was a logical choice for a route across the Monashee Mountains. This meant that the CPR had to locate a pass in the Rockies farther south than Yellowhead Pass, and find a way across the Selkirk Mountains to link that pass with Eagle Pass. The southern Rockies had not been explored since the Palliser Expedition of 1858–1859. The

Selkirk Mountains were unknown, save for the forays of Walter Moberly, Albert Perry, and a few prospectors.

The CPR executive included Canadian-born James Jerome Hill, who had moulded himself into an exemplary Yankee industrialist. Known as "the Empire Builder," Hill commanded railways, steamship lines, and coal mines. His net worth eventually reached $60 million. Hill was so pro-American, he had celebrated the signing of the CPR's charter by becoming a US citizen. Hill made finding the route through the mountains of BC the CPR's priority. To head the survey, he hired Major Albert Bowman Rogers, a fifty-two-year-old location engineer, schooled at Brown University and Yale, who had earned a reputation in the US Midwest as "the Railway Pathfinder." During the Dakota Conflict of 1862, the governor of Minnesota had commissioned Rogers a major—a title that endured as a nickname. Hill instructed Rogers to explore four passes in the Rockies, and to discover a pass across the Selkirk Mountains. If successful, Hill promised to name the Selkirk pass for Rogers, and to reward the surveyor with a cheque for five thousand dollars. (In a curious parallel, in 1869, the Legislative Council of the Colony of British Columbia and Vancouver Island had offered "$1000 to any party who will discover a suitable pass . . . through the Selkirk Mountains at not a higher

James Jerome Hill,
"The Empire Builder."

Major Albert Bowman Rogers,
"The Railway Pathfinder."

elevation than 2,500 feet." It was a lame offer, as no viable pass of such a low elevation exists.)

Rogers set to work with a brashness that grated on everyone. Portraits show a large-eyed, gaunt-faced man, whose frame barely filled his suit jacket. The wisps of his outlandish mustache touched his shoulders. To hear him speak on almost any subject was to endure a stream of cussing—punctuated with spurts of tobacco juice—traits that earned him other nicknames: "the Bishop," and "Hell's Bells Rogers."

Those who worked with Rogers initially faulted him simply for being an American assigned to a position of importance on a Canadian project. But other complaints soon mounted. Rogers had no mercy on himself. He could cover ground like a wolverine while subsisting on a diet of raw beans, bacon, hard tack, and chewing tobacco. He expected his men to do likewise. Assignments with Rogers became the dread of the CPR surveying corps. Time and again, the Major failed to learn a simple, vital lesson: that sometimes, for people engaged in hard work under difficult conditions, the difference between success and wasted seasons is the quality of their food and shelter.

It was typical of the Major that he should tackle first the most difficult part of his assignment—the unknown valleys and peaks of the Selkirk Mountains. After directing the CPR to ship five complete engineering outfits up the Missouri River and overland to the foot of the Rockies west of Fort Calgary, Rogers and his nephew, Albert Rogers, set off from Minnesota by rail for San Francisco. From there, they took steamers to Victoria and to Emory's Bar (just below Yale) in the Fraser Canyon. Following Onderdonk's railway grade and tote roads, the pair reached Fort Kamloops twenty-two days after leaving home. Rogers required another eight days to locate and hire ten Natives who would pack the gear for the exploration.

In his account of the journey, published in 1905 and contained in A. O. Wheeler's *The Selkirk Range*, Albert made a telling comment about "trying to find out how far an Indian can travel between suns with one hundred pounds on his back and no trail, [and] how little food he would require to do it." The Major could entice no volunteers, so after enlisting the help of the Jesuit missionary at Fort Kamloops, he made a contract for servitude with a chief of the Secwepemc (Shuswap) First Nation. Ten Natives would be hired and paid, but if any came back without a good report, his wages would be forfeited to the church, and the chief would administer one hundred lashes to the bare back of the offender.

Rogers not only intended to reach a height of land in the Selkirks but to carry on across the Rockies to meet his surveying outfits by July 1, 1881. The sole food the Major requisitioned for twelve men for this two-month

☆ Dollars and Sense ☆

Why would the CPR commit to an unknown route—a desperate stab across the Selkirk Mountains—when it had been common knowledge since the fur-trading days that the valley of the Columbia River looped around the north end of those mountains, offering, if not an easy route, at least a route with known evils? As is so often the case with big companies involved in big endeavours, it came down to money. Although William Cornelius Van Horne, general manager of the CPR during its construction, had serious concerns about the feasibility and safety of the Rogers Pass route, he felt the cost of operating trains on its steep grades would be less in the long term than running trains the extra seventy-seven miles around the Big Bend route in the Columbia Valley. The reduction in mileage also translated into a reduction in time: two hours for passenger trains; four hours for freight trains. As speed was everything in the argument for securing new freight traffic, Van Horne's logic made sense in 1884. However, within a few years of the railway beginning regular service, the staggering costs involved in snowshed construction and track maintenance, and the sobering losses of life in avalanches—all of which were unforeseen—revealed Rogers Pass as the more costly route for the railway.

---

trip into the unknown was 800 pounds of flour, 337 pounds of bacon, 25 pounds of baking powder, 25 pounds of salt, and 10 pounds of tea. One box of matches, a tin bucket, and two frying pans would help convert the provisions into something palatable.

On May 1, a steamer deposited the expedition at Eagle Landing on the easterly arm of Shuswap Lake. Using a canoe they found in the woods, Rogers's men began to move supplies up the Eagle River toward Eagle Pass. It took them fourteen days to cover the forty-two miles across the pass to Big Eddy on the Columbia River. They built a raft on which the Major, Albert, and the supplies ferried the river while the Natives swam and provided the propulsion.

Albert's account of the journey again turned to food: "Having learned by this time what a day's march through the average country was, as well as the capacity of the Indian appetite when unchecked, we were obliged to make a strict ration." To this point, they had travelled on rough trails. After a short jog south to the mouth of the Illecillewaet River, they began to ascend its valley, where the real hardships and rumbling of stomachs began. Albert wrote: "From now on we pushed them [the Natives], making twenty minute runs, with five minute rests, through the day. The travelling was exceedingly difficult and . . . I am convinced, but for the fear of the penalty of returning

The first difficulty in the Illecillewaet Valley for Major Rogers's 1881 expedition would have been negotiating a route around Box Canyon.

without their letters of good report, our Indians would have deserted us." Albert pushed himself, too. Of the uphill journey he wrote, "Many a time I wished myself dead."

The party required five days to cover the sixteen miles to the forks of the Illecillewaet River—where Walter Moberly had made his wrong turn in 1865—near the present-day western boundary of Glacier National Park. They were travelling through the world's only inland temperate rain forest. Stands of massive western redcedar, Douglas-fir, and western hemlock towered above them. Alder and devil's club choked the avalanche slopes. A five-foot depth of snow covered the valley floor. The snow became so soft in the warmth of the day that the men found it easier to travel in the river where it was open. In several places, they crossed bridges of avalanched snow with water 150 feet beneath them. The men supplemented their dwindling supplies by shooting caribou, mountain goats, and bears.

On May 28, the men came to another fork in the Illecillewaet River. After pitching a camp to cache what remained of the supplies, Rogers made an astute decision. Instead of following the principal stream southward to the river's source at the Illecillewaet Glacier, which would have been a railway dead end, he ascended northward alongside a mere trickle to a height of land. By keeping in the shade of the mountains and in the trees, the men travelled until 4:00 PM the next day to a level opening they hoped might be the sought-after pass. After the sun went behind the ridge to the west, the snow refroze. The men scampered across to the north edge of the clearing. Rogers was convinced they were on a watershed, but the tight valley and the dense forest did not reveal if it might serve as a railway route. Impulsively, Rogers directed his men to make an evening ascent of the east side of the valley to obtain a better view.

They kept to a strip of trees between two slide paths on the peak known today as Avalanche Mountain. Above the trees, the party took to open snow slopes. While attempting to climb a series of ledges, four of the Natives, who had fashioned a rope of sorts with their pack straps, tumbled together in a knot and out of view. To the remaining party's relief, the four soon appeared far down the slope, plunge-stepping with gusto for the valley bottom and a safe place to sleep. The eight others carried on for the crest of the ridge, which they gained as night fell.

Although the summit view convinced Rogers they had found a pass through the Selkirk Range, the immediate predicament tainted their success. Night had fallen and the men were soaking wet on a windswept ridge, with only a great rock for shelter. According to Albert Roger's account, they spent only four hours in their bivouac, but "it seemed as if those four hours outran all time."

☆ Horribly Beautiful ☆

"The walking is dreadful, we climb over and creep under fallen trees of great size and the men soon show that they feel the weight of their burdens. Their halts for rest are frequent. It is hot work for us all. The dripping rain from the bush and branches saturates us from above. Tall ferns sometimes reaching to the shoulder and Devil's clubs through which we had to crush our way make us feel as if dragged through a horsepond and our perspiration is that of a Turkish bath. We meet with obstacles of every description. The devil's clubs may be numbered by millions and they are perpetually wounding us with their spikes against which we strike. We halt frequently for rest. Our advance is varied by ascending rocky slopes and slippery masses, and again descending to a lower level. We wade through alder swamps and tread down skunk cabbage and prickly aralias [possibly thimbleberry], and so we continue until half-past four, when the tired-out men are able to go no further."

Sandford Fleming's description of travel in the Illecillewaet Valley during his crossing of Rogers Pass on foot in August 1883, in *England and Canada, A Summer Tour Between Old and New Westminister*

Devil's club (see photo on page 16) is a striking, upright shrub of the western mountains, where it grows on moist but well-drained soils at low- to mid-elevations. Where found at the bases of steep gullies, it can reach heights of more than six metres, although heights of 1.5 metres to 2.5 metres are more typical. Its large, maple-shaped leaves measure up to thirty-five centimetres across. Small, whitish flowers grow in clusters that yield shiny, flattened, red berries. The shrub is notorious for its cloak of spines that cover the stem and leaf veins (its genus name is derived from the Greek word *hoplon*, which means "weapon"). Most people find contact with the spines extremely irritating, even painful.

Cursed by white explorers (hence its species name, *horridus*), devil's club is revered by Aboriginal peoples. It has more than thirty uses among the twenty-five First Nations that live where it grows. Some of these uses are spiritual, many are medicinal. The plant is prominent in the treatment of arthritis, rheumatism, diabetes, respiratory ailments, wounds, and abdominal pain. Chemical research has confirmed that devil's club has antifungal, antiviral, antibacterial, and antimycobacterial properties. It has been used successfully in mainstream medicine to reduce the effects of diabetes, and as a cancer treatment. Devil's club is susceptible to disturbance because it takes many years to reach maturity. You may see it growing trailside on some of the walks described in Chapter Thirteen.

Devil's Club
(see page 15)

☆ Ask the Expert ☆

With a Royal Commission into the sorry affairs of what was known as the Pacific Railway on the near horizon—millions of dollars had been spent with hardly a rail laid—Sandford Fleming quit as the project's engineer-in-chief in May 1880. Rightly and wrongly, the commission subsequently blamed Fleming for the mismanagement

that had created many of the project's problems. The truth was that Fleming had been hampered from the outset by political interference. The CPR incorporated late in 1881. One of its early acts was to further salt Fleming's wounds by abandoning, in January 1882, his choice of Yellowhead Pass as the route across the Rockies. So it may seem surprising that, the following year, George Stephen, president of the CPR, sought Fleming's opinion concerning the railway's proposed new route. What is even more surprising: Fleming agreed to provide an opinion. He did this in a manner consistent with his earlier assessment of Yellowhead Pass—he travelled on foot and by horse from Kicking Horse Pass in the Rockies to Fort Kamloops, crossing Rogers Pass and Eagle Pass en route. As his companions, Fleming chose his son, Frank, and George Munro Grant, both of whom had been with him on his cross-country trip in 1872 when he had inspected the route of the Pacific Railway. Major Rogers joined the party at Golden for the crossing of Rogers Pass.

Above: In the 1870s and 1880s, Sandford Fleming cut a dashing blend between citizen of Parliament Hill and traveller of the western wilds.

Rather than descending the slope directly, at first light the half-frozen men followed the ridge south toward the peak now known as Mount Sir Donald. Driven from the ridge by the first buttress of that mountain, they descended west. The steep slope forced them to face inwards and kick steps in the snow. One of the Natives fell the last six hundred feet to the treeline. Seeing that he survived, the others promptly sat down and bum-slid down the slope. A short time later, another of the Natives dropped out of sight. Without knowing it, the party was crossing a glacier. They found the man thirty feet down, wedged between the walls of a crevasse. The men tied their pack straps together and lowered the leather thong to the man, and thus hauled him to the surface. At the cache, they found the four Natives who had survived their tumble the previous day, smoking the meat of a caribou they had killed. This served as the party's principal food as the explorers, staggering with hunger and fatigue, retraced their route to the Columbia River.

The river had risen thirty feet in less than three weeks. Rogers sent eight of the Natives across on a raft to head home to Fort Kamloops. With the other two, he and Albert departed downriver, where they eventually found other Natives who supplied a canoe, food, and a guide. After crossing into the US, Rogers discharged his remaining two servants. He and Albert made a roundabout journey to Wild Horse Camp—near the site of present-day Cranbrook, BC. The Major went north and crossed the Rockies to arrive at his surveying depot in the Bow Valley two weeks late, on July 15. Albert and two Natives headed farther north to the mouth of the Kicking Horse River, whose valley they followed east.

During the remainder of the summer, the Major ran a trial line in the Bow Valley to the eastern entrance of Kicking Horse Pass. Although Albert Rogers and his companions almost starved on their trip—requiring rescue near the head of the Kicking Horse Valley—the fact that they survived was somehow proof to the Major that Kicking Horse Pass was feasible for a railroad. At the end of 1881, the CPR executive summoned him to Montreal. The Major gave a "thumbs-up" to the Kicking Horse-Selkirk route, despite a personal knowledge gap that encompassed 128 railway miles, parts of three mountain ranges, and three of the wildest valleys in southern BC. The desperate executive took Rogers at his word and, in January 1882, stunned the country by announcing that, instead of using Yellowhead Pass as specified in its charter, the CPR would cross the Rockies by way of Kicking Horse Pass. One pass down; one to go.

After fretting the winter away, Rogers took to the mountains with customary haste in 1882. In May, the surveyor and five others departed from the site of present-day Golden to attempt to cross the Selkirks from the east. A week into the journey, they were starving when the propitious discovery of an abandoned canoe allowed them to quickly flee their predicament. After regrouping, Rogers embarked again on July 17. The going was only marginally better. For eight days his party toiled, following the Beaver River to Bear Creek (now Connaught Creek) and its sources in the Selkirks.

On July 24, Rogers gained the northern edge of the pass that he had reached the previous year. Only then did he realize the pass was not a straight shot but a high elevation S-turn through the mountains. From that day, the clearing where he stood became known as Rogers Pass. With fame and the $5,000 fortune assured, the Major returned to the Rockies to complete the survey of Kicking Horse Pass and the intervening ground along the Columbia River. (Initially, Rogers would not cash the $5,000 cheque, holding onto it and its bragging rights. Years later, William Cornelius Van Horne, when vice-president of the CPR, offered Rogers a gold watch as an enticement to cash the cheque so the company could balance its books.)

By the end of 1882, Rogers had blazed a location line through the Rockies, Selkirks, and Monashees that kept within the maximum grade allowed in the CPR's charter—2.2 percent or 116 feet per mile. But the route was

☆ Again, the Columbia ☆

The Columbia River is a riddle of hydrology. From its sources at Columbia Lake near the 49th parallel in southeastern BC, it flows 1,955 kilometres to the Pacific Ocean near the 46th parallel in Oregon. Along the way, its course variously points to every direction on the compass. The river initially flows north-northwest, captured by the Columbia Trench, the rift between the Rocky Mountains to the east and the older Columbia Mountains to the west. After 305 kilometres, the river makes a hairpin turn around the north end of the Selkirk Mountains at a place known as the Big Bend. The river then flows south between the Selkirk and Monashee mountains until it swings west again in eastern Washington state. Because the CPR crossed the Columbia Mountains, it was inevitable that the railway line would meet the Columbia River twice. The "First Crossing" was 1.3 miles west of the railway siding of Donald. The "Second Crossing" was 77.7 railway miles farther west at the confluence of the Illecillewaet River and the Columbia River; at a siding originally called Farwell, now the site of Revelstoke.

"This was then the Second Crossing, and looking round, we could see where the trail ended abruptly in the river."

Morley Roberts describing travel on the construction tote road in 1884, *The Western Avernus*

"Professor" Oliver Buell, the CPR's first official photographer, recorded this view looking north from the crest of Rogers Pass in 1886, after stepping from the luxury of a private railway car. Apart from the railway line, the pass would have looked much the same to Major Rogers in 1882. The train cars in the background probably carried ballast—crushed rock that would be used to level the uneven railbed.

This survey location crew, shown posing in the Rockies in 1884, was responsible for taking Major Rogers's line of blazes and plotting it into a workable railway grade.

impractical. The first sixteen miles west from Kicking Horse Pass ran on a sidehill, avalanche-swept in its entirety. To build the railway line on that section would have cost more than $2 million and would have required many tunnels. There were tremendous problems with the grade on the western slope of Rogers Pass, too. However, in order to maintain its financing and momentum, the CPR needed to tell Canadians it had a practical route. Half lying, half hoping, the CPR built west across the prairies in the summer of 1883, aiming track for a breach in the eastern wall of the Rockies, known as "The Gap," from where the Bow Valley led into the heart of the mountains.

☆ Farewell to Farewell ☆

In October 1883, BC Surveyor General Albert Stanhope Farwell applied to the provincial government for a land grant at the present-day site of Revelstoke. He surveyed lots and, in the custom of the day, named the paper settlement after himself. Today, A. S. Farwell's actions would have been viewed as a blatant conflict of interest. As a public servant, his employment had provided him with key knowledge that the CPR intended to build its railway line through his land

claim. Less than a month after Farwell laid his claim, the CPR registered its route with the provincial and federal governments, expecting to receive title to blocks of land adjacent to the proposed line at the site it called "Second Crossing."

When the BC government removed Farwell's lands from those allocated to the CPR, the railway objected, claiming that its charter of 1881 took precedence. Rather than bothering with an appeal or with negotiation, the CPR used the heavy-handed approach for which it would become known. It changed its route and built its station east of Farwell's holdings. Farwell resisted the inevitable. His dispute with the CPR, which lasted almost six years, greatly complicated the development of the town. In 1886, the CPR successfully requested that the Post Office change the name of the town from Farwell to Revelstoke to honour Edward Baring (whose title was Lord Revelstoke). Baring had been a principal in Baring's Bank when it had saved the CPR from bankruptcy in 1885. The CPR's will fully prevailed with the incorporation of Revelstoke on March 1, 1899.

Above: The first railway station at Revelstoke, ca. 1890.

☆ Acres of Stinking Perfection ☆

In his book written in 1884, Sandford Fleming described the Illecillewaet Valley as containing "acres of stinking perfection." The valley lies within BC's Interior Cedar-Hemlock forest zone, and is part of the world's only inland temperate rain forest. "Snow-forest" might be a more accurate description of this biome; the long-lasting winter snowpack, coupled with moderate summer rains, create a humid environment more typical of coastal locations. The damp and decay

would certainly have prompted Fleming's comment, but the greatest olfactory stimulant was probably provided by skunk cabbage, which grows in profusion in wetlands in the valley.

The striking yellow bloom of the skunk cabbage (known by the folk name, "swamp lantern") emerges from tall, hooded leaves called spathes, which themselves are remarkably coloured—burgundy with yellow mottling or stripes. The spathes conceal a space in which forms the yellow, spherical flower head, called a spadix. The actual flower of the skunk cabbage is concealed within the spadix, which never fully unfolds. The flowers have sepals but no petals. As it emerges from the recently frozen ground, the skunk cabbage emits a complex, pungent odour, which gives the plant both its folk name and its species name, *foetidus*. The odour mimics rotting flesh, and thus attracts any insects and bees that may have missed the visual flag of the plant, aiding in pollination.

Skunk cabbage emerges early from still-frozen wetlands. It accomplishes this not by force but by chemistry and by the enclosed design of the spathe. The plant generates heat—it can be as much as 20°C warmer within the spathe than outside of it. A miracle of mountain spring, skunk cabbage literally melts its way into the open. If you are visiting Rogers Pass in late spring or early summer and want to see this plant, the Skunk Cabbage boardwalk, twenty-eight kilometres east of Revelstoke on the Trans-Canada Highway, is a sure bet.

Above: Skunk Cabbage.

☆ An Alpine Spat ☆

Major Rogers grated on the Canadians in the CPR surveying corps. Their complaints were legion. Rogers was not a mountain man—he had only surveyed for railroads on the prairies. Rogers was hard on himself, his men, and their pack animals. He was stubborn, arrogant, and egocentric. The truth was a surveyor in the wilds of western Canada in 1882 needed to be as tough as railway steel to ensure his own survival and that of his men. Nonetheless, the Canadian surveyors and location engineers—fuelled in great part by jealousy that a key pass on the route had been named for Rogers—lined up to take shots at him.

One of the many acrimonious exchanges took place on the crest of Rogers Pass in 1883. James Ross, construction superintendent, had sent Charles Aeneas Shaw to check Rogers's location survey between Fort Calgary and Fort Kamloops. After a fiery meeting with Rogers at the present site of Golden, Shaw reluctantly agreed to include the Major in the crossing of the Selkirks. Along the Columbia and Beaver rivers, Shaw berated Rogers for what Shaw considered to be lousy location work. When they reached the summit of Rogers Pass, the American sought to take back some points in the exchange. According to his account in *Tales of a Pioneer Surveyor*, Rogers, gesturing to the mountains, proclaimed: "Shaw, I was the first white man ever to set eyes on this pass and this panorama." Shaw ambled over to a spring to get a drink of water, where he found the remains of a fire, some rotting tent poles, and a few rusted tin cans. He showed these to Rogers. "That's strange," replied Rogers. "I never noticed those things before. I wonder who could have camped here." Shaw was quick with his comeback. "These things were left here years ago by [Walter] Moberly when he found this pass!"

It was not true; neither Moberly nor any of his men had reached Rogers Pass. But Shaw's comment circulated widely in his day and gained currency. It may even have influenced Moberly's later account of events, in which he claimed that his assistant, Albert Perry, had reached Rogers Pass in 1866. Given how much controversy surrounded the man in his day, it is unfortunate that Major Rogers left no biographical account.

☆ The Other Rogers Pass ☆

A few years after Major Rogers's work for the CPR, James Hill hired him to survey the Rocky Mountain section of Hill's Great Northern Railroad. While Rogers was working there, his horse pitched him to the ground. He never fully recovered from his injuries, and died two years later. The name of a railway pass on the Montana-Idaho border commemorates him. It was not used on the Great Northern's route.

4
Point Man on the Pass

☆

Great enterprises require great leaders. James Jerome Hill of the CPR became patently aware of this late in 1881, a year in which his company had built only 131 miles of the transcontinental railway. Hill fired the CPR's general superintendent, replacing him with American railway wizard, William Cornelius Van Horne. The CPR could have found no better commander. Van Horne soon cleaned house. A month after his arrival at the Winnipeg field office, he dismissed the entire engineering staff. He developed a reputation for showing up everywhere and anywhere along the line as it was being built, where he badgered, cajoled, and inspired an army of workers to lay track quickly, and to solve problem after problem.

Van Horne contracted most of the work being done on the prairies in 1882 and 1883 to the Minneapolis firm of Langdon and Shepard. Despite the success of that company in meeting deadlines for completion of work, Van Horne was not entirely satisfied with the quality of the construction. The CPR formed the North American Railway Contracting Company in December 1882 to take over the remaining work in central Ontario, along the north shore of Lake Superior, and in the mountains of BC. The company hired James Worthington to supervise the central Ontario segment, John Ross to supervise the Lake Superior segment, and James Ross (no relation) to supervise work in the mountains of the west.

North American was essentially a shell company, formed by the CPR to funnel construction contracts to its backers. Its financial entanglement with the CPR was complicated and soon collapsed, leaving Van Horne, in November 1883, on the spot as his own chief contractor. Van Horne was fortunate on two counts: North American had hired fine prospects as its construction supervisors, and he had retained them after North American failed. John Ross and James Ross each faced two daunting challenges. For the former, it was the granite and the muskeg of the Canadian Shield; for the latter, it was the steep grades and the snow of the Rockies and Selkirks. In hindsight, it is clear that, of the two formidable bargains, James Ross was tagged with the tougher one.

After the 1883 construction season, Van Horne appraised the work remaining in BC. He envisioned that Andrew Onderdonk's government contract crews, who were advancing eastward along the Fraser and Thompson canyons, should have been able to lay track as far as Eagle Pass by the end of the 1885 season. That would leave a gap of 169 miles to the crest of

There could be no mistaking who was the boss: William Cornelius Van Horne in 1905.

James Ross, the CPR's western construction superintendent, faced untold hardships and monumental headaches in building the railway through the mountains, but when all was done, he possessed a countenance apparently untarnished.

On August 1, 1884, the end-of-track was at the second crossing of the Kicking Horse River in the Rockies, on the Big Hill east of Field. William MacFarlane Notman edged atop the partially completed truss work of the bridge to capture this view. In the following four months, crews laid seventy miles of track to the west and built a dozen major bridges before winter curtailed the work. This remarkable push still left the railhead a few miles short of Van Horne's goal for 1884—the foot of the Selkirks.

Kicking Horse Pass in the Rockies, where construction from the east had halted in early December 1883. It seemed reasonable that CPR crews working westward would fill that gap with rails in two years.

A year later, Van Horne must have cursed the interim result. Only seventy-three miles of track had been completed west from Kicking Horse Pass, almost thirty miles of which had been set and spiked late in the season on relatively easy ground along the Columbia River. It had taken eight months to descend the western slope of the Rockies to near the beginning of the climb to the crest of the Selkirks. How long would it take to cross those mountains to link with Onderdonk's track? Van Horne could accept only one answer: one construction season.

In January 1885, James Ross visited CPR headquarters in Montreal to assure the boss that his crews would complete the line by the end of September. Not long after his return to the Selkirks, that confidence began to wane. Ross's correspondence with Van Horne became a chronicle of complaint. In attempting to get a head start on the season, his men dealt with the tail end of a typical Selkirk winter. Temperatures of -30°F were common. Snow lay six feet deep in the valley bottom near Farwell (now Revelstoke), and nine feet deep farther up the Illecillewaet Valley. Avalanche deposits were often forty feet deep. The snow hindered logging, so there was insufficient lumber for construction. In the early going, seven men were buried in avalanches, two of them were killed. Ross reported that "the men are frightened," and showing some nerve, informed his boss that "the snow-slides on the Selkirks are much more serious than I anticipated, and I think are quite beyond your ideas of their magnitude and danger to the line." He advised Van Horne to expect an overrun of $500,000 in building the line across the Selkirks.

James Ross had based his initial assessment of the Rogers Pass work on using Major Rogers's 2.2 percent grade on the north flank of the Illecillewaet Valley. As Ross journeyed back and forth on the route, it became clear that the line was impractical. In the initial descent, the rails would have been far above the valley bottom and would have crossed avalanche slopes on Cheops Mountain with an aggregate width of almost two miles. Ross proposed that 1,400 feet of tunnels and 8,350 feet of snowsheds would be needed on that section alone. It was clear that, as soon as possible west of Rogers Pass, the line had to be taken down to the valley floor where, by routing the rails from one side of the river to the other on bridges to bypass avalanche slopes, and by using sheds and berms, the track could be better protected.

Ross had noted two tributary streams in the upper Illecillewaet Valley— Glacier Creek (the upper Illecillewaet River) and Five Mile Creek (now called Loop Brook). He imagined that by looping the track into these side valleys, the line could be lengthened and thus the grade reduced while taking the rail bed down to the valley floor. Ross had one of his construction engineers, Sammy Sykes, run a trial line. On paper, at least, the plan worked.

In a letter dated March 4, 1885, Ross recommended this new routing to Van Horne. Its selling points were not the kind that Van Horne might have wanted to hear. It lengthened the track by almost four miles; it included S-curves and total curvature equivalent to almost seven complete circles; and it incorporated four massive wooden trestles, six bridges, and fourteen snowsheds. But when compared with Major Rogers's line, the routing saved more than two hundred degrees in track curvature, while making the track safer, easier to protect from avalanches, and, remarkably, $500,000 cheaper to construct. Van Horne had walked along Rogers's line in 1884 and, although he had not seen an avalanche, he had acquired an inkling of the magnitude of the threat. He agreed to the new routing. Thus were born "The Loops"— the timber and trestle trademark of Rogers Pass.

☆ Trial by Fire ☆

Construction of the CPR had been a tumultuous process for the executive of the railway company. From eastern Canada they had watched as surveyors, engineers, and crews overcame obstacle after obstacle. Behind the scenes, two members of the executive—George Stephen and Donald Smith—had tied their extensive personal fortunes to the completion of the railway. As a result, they had run themselves to mental and physical exhaustion in dealing with banks, governments, and the forces of nature.

Because of the snowshed construction and track ballasting required in the mountains, through traffic on the CPR began later than hoped for in 1886. It therefore must have been with great relief that Stephen and Smith received the news from Van Horne on July 4, 1886, that the CPR's first transcontinental passenger train, the Pacific Express, had arrived on time at Port Moody, BC. Imagine, then, Stephen's and Smith's dismay, when informed by a telegram three days later that the second train to reach the west coast had suffered disaster on its return across the country.

According to Harry Abbott, the CPR's superintendent of mountain operations, the second Atlantic Express made a hazardous descent from Rogers Pass to Beavermouth in the early afternoon of July 7: "The whole country being ablaze, a fierce fire raging and a perfect hurricane blowing at the time, and all telegraph wires down." When the train emerged from Beaver Canyon, fire surrounded the track. The engineer stopped the train so the conductor could walk ahead to converse with the section gang, who were hosing down stacks of locomotive cordwood. The men told the conductor the track was clear for the short run to Beaver station. The train inched ahead, but when it came alongside two piles of wood near the station wye, one of the piles—evidently on fire—toppled onto the track just after locomotive 354 had passed, derailing the coal and baggage cars.

The track and surroundings were soon engulfed. The passengers, a locomotive, and the first class sleeping car were saved by the prompt action of the train crew, whose efforts Abbott later reviewed with a mixture of praise and contempt. The locomotive fireman was burned as he escaped. The baggage man could not open the baggage car because the door was blocked by burning wood. The paymaster left $10,000 to burn and was criticized for being "thoroughly unnerved," whereas the mail clerk got all the mail off the train despite receiving burns to his arms and legs.

The fire destroyed the baggage car, a sleeping car, a coach, the station house, and a telegraph office. It was a bad day all around. Because the telegraph system was down, prompt word of the calamity could not be communicated to Donald station, the closest source of help. Yet, it might not have mattered. At

With a drop of more than 200 feet beneath them, a bridge gang pose near the centre of the Stoney Creek bridge at its completion in the second week of August 1885. The occasion might have been cause for celebration but the men bear expressions of relief. At least two construction workers fell to their deaths from the bridge deck. It seems likely that the fearless photographer set up the shot on the boom of a crane.

noon that day, according to Abbott, "a tornado struck Donald and had [tree] clearing [previously] not been done to a considerable distance all around, the place would have been destroyed by fire." When help did arrive from Donald, it was some six hours after the Atlantic Express had met grief. By this time, fire raged all along the Beaver Valley from Beavermouth to Stoney Creek. The foreman of the Stoney Creek section gang made an urgent trip by handcar to Beaver station to report that he needed help to save the bridges up-valley. With the situation at Beaver station barely under control and the track repaired, a locomotive and men were dispatched. Surprise Creek bridge caught fire three times later that day and each time was extinguished. If the CPR had not previously cleared the forest at trackside to create firebreaks, it seems a certainty that most of the bridges in the Beaver Valley would have been lost in what can only be described as a firestorm, the likes of which has not been seen along the CPR since.

Perhaps staving off the inevitable question from Van Horne, Abbott reported to his boss that, during the debacle, the passengers of the Atlantic Express had been "comfortably placed, and supplied with meals." However, Abbott could not candy-coat the obvious: The CPR's difficulties had not ended with the completion of track; the trials of operating a railway in the mountains had only just begun.

5
The Loops

The principle behind the construction of The Loops was a simple one that previously had been employed with success on railways in Europe and in the western US: double the length of a section of track to reduce the grade by one-half. Thus, if the grade averaged 4.5 percent over four miles of valley bottom—as it did immediately west of Rogers Pass—it would average 2.25 percent if eight miles of track could be squeezed into that distance. The challenges west of Rogers Pass were finding the space while keeping a consistent grade and protecting the track from avalanches.

Given the many inflexibilities of the terrain, the CPR was fortunate that two valleys offered small bays into which it could loop the line. The first of these was the upper reach of the Illecillewaet River itself (called Glacier Creek during CPR construction), where it curved south toward its source at the Illecillewaet Glacier. The second was the mouth of Loop Brook (then called Five Mile Creek because it was five railway miles from the crest of Rogers Pass), where it entered the Illecillewaet Valley from the south. Two sets of curves did not lengthen the line sufficiently. However, taking the track south into Five Mile Creek provided room on the north side of the Illecillewaet Valley to make a third loop on the valley floor.

A westbound train leaving Rogers Pass travelled southeast to the beginning of a sweeping turn of more than 180 degrees that had a radius of approximately six hundred yards. It made its first crossing of the Illecillewaet River (Glacier Creek) just before Glacier House. After it passed this hotel,

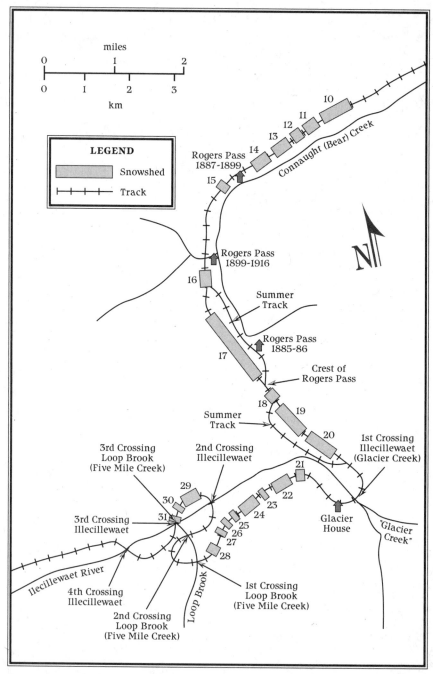

Rogers Pass and The Loops, 1885–1916.

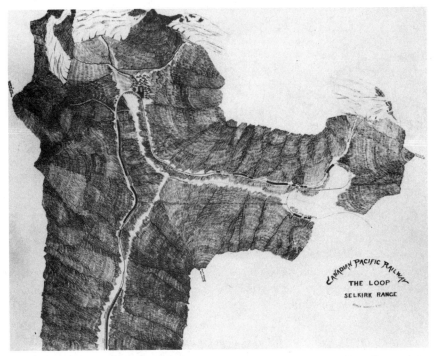

North is at the bottom and east is on the left in this official plan of The Loops.
The snowsheds are shown in black. The dotted, horizontal line near the centre of the
diagram is 1.5 miles long, connecting points that are 4.25 miles apart on the rails.

the train headed northwest. A sharp turn of almost 90 degrees took the train along the southern flank of the Illecillewaet Valley for just over one mile, through sheds 21-28, to the mouth of Loop Brook (Five Mile Creek). The track curved south into the tributary valley, and then west to cross the creek again, then north and northeast to cross the creek yet again—a near complete circle, this time with a radius of only four hundred yards. Just after the track straightened, it began a sharp turn north (making its second crossing of the Illecillewaet River), then west through sheds 29-31, and southwest (making its third crossings of both Loop Brook and the Illecillewaet River), tracing a near complete circle with a radius of about five hundred yards. The westernmost points of the second and third parts of The Loops were within three hundred yards of each other in a straight line, but were 2.5 miles apart along the track, with an elevation difference of some 280 feet.

To railroaders and passengers alike, The Loops were an engineering marvel. Because the structures were much photographed, there exists a fairly complete record of their modifications. At first, the principle work done on The Loops was timber replacement on the trestles, and snowshed

This is the second crossing of Loop Brook. This trestle was replaced by the stone pillars visible today on the south side of the Trans-Canada Highway. Mount Bonney is in the distant background.

For photographers of the day, the most popular viewpoint for The Loops involved a scramble onto the lower slope of Ross Peak to look east (railway-west) along the trestle at the second crossing of Loop Brook. (This trestle is the same as in the previous image, but viewed from the opposite end). Today, the Trans-Canada Highway is just left of the trestle. Various archives contain more than twenty

variations on this view, taken between 1887 (when this image was taken) and 1916. Many photographers followed William Macfarlane Notman's lead, captioning this scene: "The Loop, showing four tracks." The scar on the lower slopes of Uto Peak (centre background) is the railway grade between Rogers Pass and Glacier House, angling down to the right. In the middle distance on the right, in the trees, the grade just above the first crossing of Loop Brook is visible. The roof of 29 Shed is visible at the base of the avalanche slope on the left-hand edge of the photo. This was the only place in Canada where four elements of the CPR main line, each oriented in a different direction, could be seen from one viewpoint. No such location exists today.

William Macfarlane Notman's large format photographs contain remarkable detail. This enlargement of the area at the far end of the trestle in the previous image shows

the trackside accommodation for the watchman responsible for The Loops. The watchman could either walk the track to inspect the trestles, or take shortcuts—a trail runs across the railway line, between the shack and the end of the trestle. This trail would have led uphill (right) to the first crossing of Loop Brook and downhill (left) to the third crossing of Loop Brook and the third crossing of the Illecillewaet River. The water barrel on the left side of the railway track was one of half a dozen on the trestle intended to provide primitive fire protection. At some locations, culverts funnelled streams into pipes that fed the barrels—it appears that such a system may have been in place on this trestle. The watchman could use the barrel water to put out spot fires caused by passing locomotives.

This view, taken railway-west of the previous image at the third crossing of the Illecillewaet River, shows three levels of track. In the background on the left, the track angles downhill from Glacier House to the first crossing of Loop Brook, with its trestle just visible in the background on the right. The second crossing of Loop Brook is in the middle distance, just right of centre. From the left end of that trestle, the track embankment is visible, extending to the left edge of the photograph. Just out of view on the left, the track curved toward the camera at the second crossing of the river. Note how the piers of the foreground trestle (which spans the Illecillewaet River and the mouth of Loop Brook) diminish in height toward the west (right)—to keep the track on the required grade.

The rough edges of construction were gone and the days of The Loops were numbered when this image was taken in 1909. It shows steel trestles on stone pillars at the third crossing of the Illecillewaet River (right foreground), with the second crossing of the river and the western portal of 31 Shed (lower left centre). Snowsheds 24–27 are in the background, along with the unmistakable spire of Mount Sir Donald.

reconstruction to repair each winter's damage. By 1897, as train traffic became more frequent and locomotives more powerful and heavier, the CPR began to fill the trestles to strengthen them. The gradients of Five Mile Creek and Glacier Creek were insufficient to permit hydraulic filling, as had been carried out at Mountain Creek (see pages 46-47) east of Rogers Pass. Instead, the CPR used gondola dump cars to pile mountains of fill beneath the trestles.

However, this method proved insufficient, so the CPR began an ambitious project to replace the wooden trestles on The Loops with steel trusses resting atop stone pillars. European masons began the stonework in the early 1900s and completed the job in 1906 without major closures of the line. It was expensive work for its day. The replacement of the trestle at the second crossing of the Illecillewaet River cost $76,500. To walk The Loops trail today is to

It is difficult to comprehend the scope, the danger, and the hardship of the work involved in the construction of the mighty stone pillars of The Loops. The masons laboured for almost six years with train traffic over their heads, creating what now endure as monuments to human industry and ingenuity. The pillars are the oldest surviving examples of this kind of architecture in western Canada. Parks Canada carries out vegetation maintenance to help preserve the pillars. This is the first crossing of Loop Brook, looking south.

marvel that the project was even conceived, let alone carried out. It is also to marvel at the fortitude of the CPR, which committed to the project even as it was seriously contemplating the construction of the Connaught Tunnel. A decade after the reconstruction of The Loops, the tunnel would relegate all that expense and the magnificent stone pillars to railroad history.

☆ Helpers, Howes, and Wyes ☆

Patented by William Howe of Spencer, Massachusetts in 1840, the Howe truss became the prototypical North American railroad bridge in the mid- to late-1800s. Its popularity stemmed from its relative strength over long spans. Howe's bridge design incorporated wooden upper and lower chords, and wooden diagonals, secured with vertical iron tie rods. With more wooden than steel components, it was ideal for construction in remote, forested locations.

Although it was relatively economical and strong, the Howe truss has been cited as the leading cause of railroad deaths in its era. It was a minimalistic

design, with the characteristic that if one bridge component failed, the entire structure would collapse. Haphazard loads on trains often damaged the wooden members, loosening the iron rods to where they would project and be hit by other trains. Successive episodes of damage would weaken the structure to the point where it would collapse, usually under the weight of a train. Howe truss spans were also susceptible to fire. A railroad that did not constantly inspect and repair Howe trusses did so at its own peril. Howe, himself, came from a family of inventors. Elias Howe, a relative, secured the first US patent for a sewing machine.

To turn its work locomotives around, the CPR built turntables at its major division points in the Rockies and Selkirks, and at stations that served as local operational hubs—Canmore, Laggan (Lake Louise), Field, Golden, Donald, Albert Canyon, Rogers Pass, and Revelstoke. Crews serviced the locomotives in adjacent roundhouses. To make more economical use of helper locomotives on the steep grades between these points, the CPR also installed sections of siding track known as wyes. By going forward on one leg of a wye and then reversing down the other leg (or vice versa), crews could turn a locomotive or a short train, saving the time and distance required to reach the nearest turntable. The CPR installed wyes at Stephen, Leanchoil, Beavermouth, Stoney Creek, and at the new Glacier station after the Connaught Tunnel opened in 1916. In the tight terrain, the Glacier wye ended in a shed that butted against the run out of an avalanche slope.

Above: The Howe truss span over Skuzzy Creek in the Fraser Canyon, ca. 1884.

In this view of the twelve-stall roundhouse and turntable at Donald in the late 1880s, the cordwood tender for Consolidation-type locomotive 403 is visible in the fifth stall from the left. Another Consolidation-type locomotive (probably 401, 402, or 403, as the four were delivered as a series) is on the turntable. These Consolidations entered service between September 1886 and January 1887 and were in Class SD, the second batch of Consolidations built by the CPR specifically for helper work in the mountains. They had 2-8-0 wheel configurations and fifty-one-inch diameter driving wheels. In 1907, locomotive 403 was renumbered as 1302 when converted from coal-fired to oil-fired. The CPR scrapped it in 1909. Locomotives 402 and 404 served as coal-burners until scrapped in 1907. Locomotive 401 was the longest serving of the four. It was renumbered as 1300 in 1907, and as 3100 in 1913. The CPR scrapped it in 1922.

In another view of the Donald roundhouse from the same era (probably 1887), locomotive 376, its tender heaped with cordwood, is ready for duty. The stalls house three other Standard American-type, 4-4-0 helper locomotives, including 381 and 374. Locomotive 374 pulled the first passenger train to reach the new end of track in Vancouver in May 1887. It saw service with the CPR for 59 years and is now preserved and on display at the Roundhouse Community Centre in Vancouver.

☆ Making the Grade ☆

Gravity, momentum, and resistance are each at times allies and opponents of railway operations. The ideal grade for a railway is straight and level; fuel costs and mechanical wear are minimal, while the relative payload capacity is greater. In North America, railway grades are measured in percent. One foot of elevation change in one hundred feet of line (fifty-two feet of elevation change in one mile) equates to a grade of 1 percent. Grades of 0.1 to 0.4 percent are the mark of ideal terrain or a superbly engineered railroad. Grades of 1.0 to 1.5 percent are considered steep. Those of 1.5 to 2.2 percent are considered heavy and are to be avoided. Grades of 2.2 to 3.3 percent are extreme.

The limiting grade on a section of track is called the ruling grade. It may not be the absolute steepest grade on that section. Trains might be able to negotiate short, steeper climbs with the momentum gained from an adjacent downhill grade. However, in most cases, if the ruling grade is heavy, it dictates where, and how many, helper locomotives will need to be added to a train, or whether the train should be split and taken up the grade in sections. The ruling grade also becomes a factor for downhill-bound trains as it dictates how many helper locomotives must be added to assist with braking.

Curves in the track create resistance due to the increased friction that results from the centrifugal force between the wheel flanges and the rails. Where curves are located on inclines, the factors that hinder locomotive performance compound rapidly. Location engineers "compensate" for curvature by attempting to decrease an uphill grade immediately prior to a curve. This reduction is typically on the order of 0.2 to 0.3 percent and is achieved by cutting into the terrain.

Track curvature is measured in degrees of arc traversed for each one hundred feet of track. (A circle contains 360 degrees.) Location engineers strive to keep curves to less than two degrees, but in the mountains, curves of 5 to 10 degrees are necessarily common. The theoretical maximum curve that a modern diesel-electric locomotive can negotiate is twenty degrees. The sharpest curve on the CPR main line today is the twelve-degree "Macdonald curve" in the Illecillewaet Valley west of Rogers Pass. For a short time in the early 1900s, the CPR operated a sixteen-degree curve in the lower Kicking Horse Canyon in the Rockies. This was the sharpest curve ever run on a Canadian railroad.

The dreaded combination of railway operations is a reverse curve on a grade—an S-shaped curve, where the lead locomotive will be, in effect, heading in a different direction from the midsection of the train. Between Donald and Beavermouth, BC, on the eastern approach to Rogers Pass, the original alignment of the CPR incorporated a reverse curve comprised of a ten-degree

This reverse curve on a steep grade, with a short intervening section of straight track, typifies the bane of mountain railroading. Note the cross-elevation of the distant curve. CP staff photographer, Nicholas Morant, captured this view in the Illecillewaet Valley.

curve separated from an opposing eight-degree curve by only seventy feet of straight track.

A super-elevated curve is one where the outside rail is higher relative to the inside rail to allow a train to take the curve at greater speed. Engineers call this difference the cross-elevation. It can be as much as six inches on a shallow curve. (The rails on a track measure four feet and eight and one-half inches apart.) Super-elevated curves were removed from many railways after the decline of relatively high-speed passenger trains in the 1960s and 1970s. Their absence has become a limiting factor in some proposed reintroductions of passenger service.

6

Bridges over Troublesome Waters

Today, Canadian Pacific operates more than 3,500 bridges, with an aggregate length of eighty-five miles. The company learned much about the science and craft of building and maintaining its bridges from its early experiences on the eastern approach to Rogers Pass. Many of these lessons did not come easily.

From Golden, BC, the surveyed line of the CPR followed the Columbia River northwest for 28.2 miles to its confluence with the Beaver River near Beavermouth, elevation 2,458 feet. From there, the line made a sharp turn to the southwest into the Beaver River valley. In the ensuing 19.8-mile climb along the west slope of the valley and to the railway crest of Rogers Pass (4,351 feet), the line gained 1,893 feet, producing an average grade of 1.81 percent (95.6 feet per mile), with a maximum or "ruling grade" of 2.2 percent that ran for 4.4 miles. Then, as now, this was extreme terrain for a railroad.

Another aspect of the landscape made this section of track problematic for the CPR. The Beaver River valley occupies a geologic rift between the Purcell Mountains to the east, and the southern Selkirk Mountains to the west. The division between the two ranges is the Beaver Fault, in which the bedrock on the west side of the valley drops downward relative to the bedrock on the east side. As is often the case, the resulting fault valley is deeply eroded,

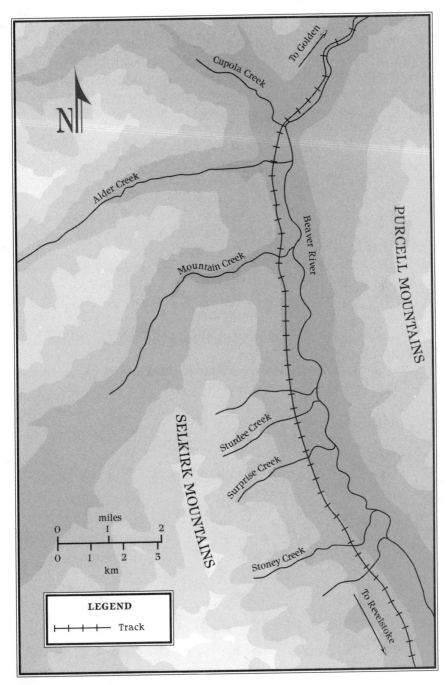

The Beaver River valley in 1885.

creating steep side slopes, especially on its western flank. This required extensive cutting of embankments and filling of hollows to create the rail bed. But the greatest trials for James Ross, construction superintendent for the CPR, came where tributary streams, plummeting from slopes to the west, bisected the grade. There were a dozen such crossings in 14.2 miles. Three of these in the space of 5.4 miles toward the south end of the climb—Mountain Creek, Surprise Creek, and Stoney Creek—posed construction challenges of such magnitude they almost scuttled the railway.

The three creeks were ravine-like where they crossed the grade. The resulting heights of the bridge decks above their creeks were 154 feet at Mountain Creek, 180 feet at Surprise Creek, and 273.2 feet at Stoney Creek. There was only one higher railway bridge in the world in 1885—the deck of Gustave Eiffel's newly completed Garabit Viaduct in France rose four hundred feet above the Truyére River. However, none of its six support towers was as high as the central tower of the Stoney Creek bridge (228.2 feet), and the Garabit towers were made of steel. So, CPR workers and construction engineers claimed their structure was the highest railway bridge in the world and, if challenged on this claim, added with emphasis that it was the highest *wooden* bridge. The combined length of the decks of the three principal Beaver Valley bridges was 1,944 feet.

James Ross estimated that between four million and five million board feet of locally felled lumber went into the structures. (A "typical" modern,

The CPR's first official photographer, Oliver Buell, was on hand to photograph the last stages of construction of the Stoney Creek bridge in 1885. This close-up shows diagonal bracing between the piers, with the centre span a few trusses from completion.

The completed Mountain Creek bridge was probably the largest wooden structure in the world at the time. Oliver Buell took this view to the south in May 1886, a month before regular passenger service traffic began. Note the people at the trackside.

Sawmills, such as this one near Stoney Creek, sprang up along the CPR right-of-way in the Selkirk Mountains to feed the construction of bridges and snowsheds. The sawyers had their pick of giant, old-growth specimens of some of the finest timber-producing, softwood species on the planet: western redcedar, Douglas-fir, Engelmann spruce, lodgepole pine, western hemlock, and mountain hemlock.

wood frame home requires fifteen thousand board feet.) The Mountain Creek bridge alone consumed more than two million board feet. It may have been the largest wooden structure built up to that time.

The bridge sites became construction bottlenecks, delaying the shipment of supplies to points farther west, so the CPR pushed crews to complete the structures with remarkable haste. Workers finished the Mountain Creek bridge in early May 1885 before all the snow was gone from the valley bottom. They completed the last bridge, at Stoney Creek, at the end of the first week of August. It took nine days to lay track the remaining distance to the crest of the pass, which was reached on August 17.

In a letter to William Cornelius Van Horne, Ross certified the soundness of the bridges: "[T]hey have all been difficult structures, but they are as good as can be made in wood. I will guarantee them for 'Consolidated,' [Consolidation, 2-8-0] or 'Decapod' or any similar class of engine you wish to run over them." Ross had sited the bridge towers on bedrock wherever possible, but the central tower of the Stoney Creek bridge had to be placed on cribbing that was pummelled by the creek.

The bridges, built on grades of almost 2 percent, terrified construction workers and train crews. When Van Horne arrived to inspect work in 1885, the engineer of one construction train voiced concern about the safety of the Stoney Creek bridge. Van Horne replied, "Here, get down and I'll take her over myself." When approaching the Mountain Creek bridge with the boss still in the cab, the engineer quipped: "If you ain't afraid of getting killed Mr. Van Horne, with all your money, I ain't afraid either." Van Horne responded: "We'll have a double funeral—at my expense of course."

Although they were structurally sound at the outset, the bridges had an Achilles heel—fire. The CPR received a taste of the peril even before all the bridges were completed. In early May 1885, the centre of the 150-foot span at the mouth of the Beaver River burned when embers fell from a forest fire nearby. Ross wrote again to Van Horne: "These high wooden bridges in the Selkirks will have to be closely watched. I consider it would be a good idea to put a tank at a large bridge like Mountain Creek and have two lines of pipe run over it, with [stop]cocks to be used during the dry season." The summer of 1885 was exceptionally dry, but, strapped for time and resources, the CPR put no such precautions in place. In July, a forest fire consumed fourteen boxcars of lumber destined for the trusses of the Stoney Creek bridge. Logging crews worked around the clock to produce replacement lumber. On July 7, 1886, the CPR's first year of transcontinental operation, the Surprise Creek bridge caught fire three times as a firestorm swept the Beaver Valley (see Trial by Fire on pages 27-28).

Ross, his design engineers, and his construction crews had done their

For more than 120 years, the iconic Stoney Creek bridge has drawn photographers to vantage points on, below, and above its span. Photographer R. H. Trueman ascended the slope upstream from the bridge at its north (railway-east) end to take this view that shows the original bridge in the early 1890s. The train consists of eight cars, with one road locomotive, and a helper coupled at the rear. The caboose is out of view behind the helper. The CPR later abandoned the practice of coupling helpers directly behind passenger cars, after learning the hard way that, when a helper engineer misjudged the power requirements, the locomotive could plough ahead into the passenger compartment. The steam plumes in this view indicate a time exposure of a stationary train. The helper engineer is looking at the camera, so it appears that the train was being held on the bridge—a common concession for professional photographers in the early days of the CPR.

Judging by the collar of the man standing in front of the left-hand cabin, it may have been a Sunday when this photograph was taken. H. Swan, in front of the right-hand cabin (perhaps with a Bible in his hands), was the engineer in charge of building the Stoney Creek bridge. His crew's camp was in the creek bed below the bridge site. It would have been a tough uphill commute in the morning, but the cabins were blessed with running water and no shortage of firewood.

best building the massive bridges, but the increasing weight of locomotives, the greater number and size of freight trains, and the perpetual risk of fire forced the CPR to take action. With the steep creeks nearby, the lofty bridges were ideal for the application of hydraulic filling, a technology borrowed from placer mining. By diverting creek water into spillways, into which workers dumped rock and soil, engineers were able to direct sluices of watery fill around the bridge piers and trestle works. For cribbing, the CPR used old railway ties, tree trunks, and large boulders. When the water trickled out, the fill set up like concrete within the barriers.

Hydraulic filling was a brilliant solution that strengthened the bridge approaches, however, the wooden central spans still required steel rein-forcement. The Stoney Creek bridge was first. Its central span was replaced in 1893 with a 336-foot-long, three-hinged steel arch, flanked by two truss spans that brought the total length of the bridge to 484 feet. At 307 feet above the creek, it remained the CPR's highest bridge until completion of the 314-foot-high Lethbridge Viaduct on the Crowsnest line in 1909. The original Stoney Creek bridge had occupied the only sound footing in the gorge, so

Using hydraulic filling, the CPR created 230,000 cubic yards of fill at the Mountain Creek bridge site at a cost of roughly seven cents per cubic yard—less than half of what it would have cost to do the same work with a steam shovel and dump cars.

The hydraulic filling of the Mountain Creek bridge was complete, and the central span had been replaced with steel, when this photo was taken in 1900. Two years later, the entire bridge was steel.

the CPR built the new bridge around the old bridge without interrupting traffic. This was accomplished by a complicated and ingenious method that used cantilevers and bracing. Eventually, the old and new arches were yoked together with equal loading. When tested with four locomotives totalling 1,100 tons, the new bridge deflected a mere 1.625 inches.

Unlike the Stoney Creek bridge, the CPR built the second Surprise Creek bridge just downstream from the first. It included a 290-foot-long central span (the total bridge length was 453 feet), with work completed in 1896. The replacement of the Mountain Creek bridge was accomplished over several years ending in 1902. It essentially became a 585-foot-long steel trestle. With its approaches filled, it was a much less impressive structure than its predecessor.

As freight traffic increased and locomotives became more powerful, the typical weight of locomotives climbed, from 458,000 pounds in 1915, to 504,000 pounds in 1920, and then to 750,000 pounds with the introduction

In 1893, crews constructed the steel skeleton of the second Stoney Creek bridge around the original wooden trestles and piers.

Rebuilt in 1929, the Stoney Creek bridge is still in use today.

This view from 1893 shows a riveting crew near centre span during reconstruction of the Stoney Creek bridge, with a drop of more than two hundred feet beneath them. The daring photographer was probably on a boom that extended from the bridge.

of the Selkirk-type locomotives in 1929. Rather than replace the Mountain Creek and Stoney Creek bridges, the CPR chose to reinforce them with steel in 1928-1929. At the same time, the CPR began to build a third Surprise Creek bridge at the location of the first bridge. Unfortunately, work on the bridge began too late, and a tragedy soon followed.

☆ A Deadly Surprise ☆

The second bridge over Surprise Creek saw use from 1896 until a sad day in January 1929. The mountains were in the grip of an Arctic air mass that pushed temperatures at Rogers Pass to -40°F—weather that crippled the operation of steam locomotives. A succession of equipment failures, on the tail of a scheduling mistake, led to a deadly assignment for two helper locomotives from Beavermouth.

On January 28, westbound passenger train Number 3 arrived at Beavermouth to discover that the dispatcher had forgotten to assign a helper locomotive and crew to take the train over Rogers Pass. The first helper crew to respond found that the boiler of its locomotive was leaking, and so declined the assignment. (In those days, crews were dedicated to specific locomotives.) The delay that resulted while another crew responded with engine 5779 contributed to problems with the road locomotive, engine 5158. When underway again on the climb to the pass, 5158 broke down and was cut out of the train. While engine 5779 held the train on the grade, a second helper, locomotive 5767, was dispatched to take the place of engine 5158. With some difficulty, the two helpers took the train over the rest of the climb and through the Connaught Tunnel to Glacier station, where a helper from Revelstoke took command. Locomotives 5779 and 5767— both Decapod-type, Class R3c, with 2-10-0 wheel configurations—were turned on the wye to run "light" (without an assignment) back to Beavermouth.

Descending the grade at six miles per hour at 7:45 AM, engine 5779, with 5767 coupled behind it, led the way onto the 455-foot span of the Surprise Creek bridge. Engineer Doug Fraser and fireman Bill Alison later told of how the bridge creaked as they crossed it. Apparently, this was not unusual in cold weather. As 5779 was about to clear the bridge, Fraser heard a bang from behind and felt a sharp backwards tug. He gave 5779 full power. When certain that 5779 and 5767 would be off the deck, Fraser stopped 5779 and applied the brake. He and Alison looked back to discover that the rear wheels of 5779's tender were resting on the ground. The track behind had disappeared, as had a section of the bridge and engine 5767 with its crew, engineer Bert Woodland and fireman Jeffrey Griffiths.

Fraser sent Alison down the grade to the Sturdee siding to make a telegraph report to the dispatcher in Revelstoke. Fraser climbed down into the canyon but, because of the heat from the ruptured locomotive boiler, he could not approach within thirty feet of the wreck of 5767. It seemed a certainty that the crew must have been killed, so Fraser climbed out of the other side of the canyon to place warning flares before walking the three miles uphill to Stoney Creek siding, where he arrived exhausted. When Alison returned from Sturdee, he also climbed

The wreck of locomotive 5767 and the ruin of the second Surprise Creek bridge.

down to the wreck. The heat had subsided. He found Woodland's body outside the locomotive. Griffiths's corpse was pinned inside. Railway employees and the residents of Revelstoke reeled from the tragedy, the second fatal accident on the Rogers Pass grade in two days. The earlier incident, a head-on collision between two trains, had also claimed two lives.

The accident happened on a Monday. The jury of a coroner's inquest convened on the Wednesday and returned a verdict of "accidental death" on the Saturday. Its only recommendation was that the CPR inspect its bridges with greater frequency than the fourteen months that had lapsed at Surprise Creek.

The CPR and its contractors surveyed the bridge and inventoried the damage. The bottom chord of the south arch was broken, the main arch was broken at the south end and three feet out of alignment, and the east flanking span was broken in two places and hanging from pins. The CPR had poured concrete footings in the summer of 1928 to support a new bridge slated for construction in the summer of 1929. The two construction companies involved advised against any kind of temporary repair to the old bridge. So, the CPR committed to the longest voluntary line closure in its history. Beginning on January 31, 1929, and working around the clock until February 17, crews replaced the Surprise Creek bridge with a steel arch structure designed to accommodate the weight of the Selkirk-type locomotives then being introduced. Design engineer P. B. Motley had supervised the drawings for the 1896 bridge and, in a curious circumstance, was the engineer who set off the charges that demolished the wreck of that bridge in 1929. Bill Alison was the fireman on one of the helper locomotives on the first train across the new bridge. Locomotive 5767 was removed from the creek in three pieces but, remarkably, was refitted for service. The CPR finally scrapped it in 1956.

7

The Rule
of Winter

Following completion of the CPR on November 7, 1885, only one railway car travelled across the country before Vice-President William Cornelius Van Horne shut down the route between Calgary and Kamloops for the winter. The train's journey was a publicity stunt to prove the CPR was in business as a transcontinental railway. The car contained a shipment of forty drums of oil from the Halifax naval base for delivery to the Esquimault naval base on Vancouver Island. The oil began its journey on October 9 and was held in Quebec City, awaiting completion of the line in BC. On November 16, the shipment moved west on regular freight trains. From Moose Jaw, Saskatchewan, to Port Moody, BC, it ran as a special train, the Naval Supply Extra. The journey from Quebec took six and a half days.

With the point proven, Van Horne knew there was nothing to be gained by running trains through the winter on incompletely ballasted track that was unprotected from avalanches. To help gather information about the work that would be required to shield the rails from the threat, Van Horne assigned three division engineers to spend the winter of 1885–1886 in camps near Rogers Pass. They were to observe avalanche activity, plot the sites of snowsheds, and make site-specific suggestions for the structures required. Van Horne probably assumed that whatever work the engineers decreed necessary

could be completed in the spring of 1886 to allow prompt establishment of regular passenger and freight service to the west coast. Although the CPR was open for business year-round as far west as Calgary, it sorely needed a broader revenue base.

During the winter of 1885–1886, construction engineer Granville Cuningham occupied an observation camp at Raspberry Creek, just east of Rogers Pass. He documented mind-boggling avalanche activity. Cuningham estimated that one slide deposit, which covered 1,800 feet of track, held 120,000 cubic yards of snow. At another location, nine separate avalanches covered the line. Another avalanche pile was thirty-nine feet deep. Cuningham's colleagues, construction engineers by the names of Ellson and Chisholm, reported similar findings west of the pass.

In June 1886, after the CPR's engineering department had digested the reports, it timidly presented Van Horne with plans and a financial estimate of the required work. This was about the time the boss had been wanting the construction finished. Van Horne must have hit the roof. The budget was $1,126,034—almost 1 percent of what it had cost to build the railway between central Ontario and the BC coast. The engineering department was calling for nineteen million board feet of lumber to be used to construct fifty-four snowsheds that, collectively, would cover more than five miles of track between a point six miles east of Rogers Pass and Three Valley, 15.5 miles west of Revelstoke. Thirty-one of the sheds were to be constructed in the fifteen miles between Bear Creek and Ross Peak. The longest snowshed, at 3,130 feet, would be 17 Shed on the crest of Rogers Pass. (Ultimately, the CPR spent $1,600,000 on the structures—more than sixty dollars per linear foot of snowshed.)

Van Horne knew two things: The work would never be completed in one season, and the sheds would detract from the experience of passengers by blocking mountain views. His only remedy for the first problem was to incur more expense by adding snow removal crews the following winter. To counter the second problem, Van Horne laid summer track to bypass many of the sheds.

When completed in 1887, the shed system was a success, but one that required modification and constant maintenance while introducing its own set of headaches. Some of the sheds were not long enough. The following winter, avalanched snow spilled around shed ends, plugging the track. Snow and boulders crushed other sheds. Some sections of track, not swept by avalanches in the winters of 1885, 1886, and 1887, were buried in subsequent winters. The sheds were fire traps, threatened by sparks from locomotives and by forest fires. Van Horne posted watchmen at trackside cabins to guard against fires. Pipes running from streams on the slopes above carried

At 3,130 feet, 17 Shed was the longest in Rogers Pass and on the CPR line. It was under construction when William Macfarlane Notman took this photograph in the summer of 1886, probably while standing atop a rail car. Most of 17 Shed had already been "buried" to strengthen it. (You can see the shed curving to the left in the mid-background.) Summer track is to the left of the shed. The construction tote road is on the extreme left. Today's Trans-Canada Highway roughly follows the tote road's route. In the background on the left, the buildings of the first Rogers Pass station are at trackside.

This view shows the same scene as is in the previous image, approximately eighteen years later. A jungle-like growth of alder and other shrubs masks most of the construction scars. A few tents are pitched between the tote road, at the left edge of the photo, and the railway line. The buildings at trackside, visible in the background of the previous image, are long gone.

This is an early view looking north from the roof of 19 Shed, the second longest in Rogers Pass, with Mt. Sifton in the background. Summer track has not yet been laid alongside the shed.

This Vaux family photograph, taken on August 13, 1898, is a reverse view of the image above. It shows a crew rebuilding the northerly segment of the shed after an avalanche the previous winter. Summer track is on the right. The Great Glacier is in the background.

Landscape features and track routing dictated the styles and the shapes of the snowsheds. CPR engineers developed at least nine basic shed designs, each specifically intended to withstand a slide from one side of a valley, a slide from both, or a slide falling almost vertically onto the roof. The CPR tucked some sheds into the valley walls, hoping that most of the sliding snow would overshoot the structures. But at least one of the sheds was seventy feet wide. The 12" x 15" shed bents were hewn from Douglas-fir timbers and were typically placed on five-foot centres. The CPR often salvaged lumber that had been sawn out of bridge decks to use for shed cribbing.

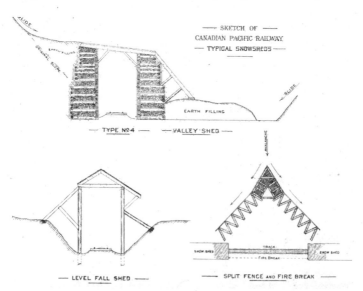

This illustration contains elevation views of two snowshed designs and a plan view of a firebreak and accompanying diversion fence.

Construction of the Rogers Pass snowsheds lasted almost two years and was only completed in that time by pushing the technical limits of construction and the endurance of workers. Here, men labour in winter conditions to create a cut, bracing, and snowshed on the western approach to Rogers Pass, with the Illecillewaet River below, avalanche slopes all around, and comfort forty miles away. The men in the foreground are standing on the roof timbers of a partially completed shed.

The Rogers Pass snowshed construction was demanding, dangerous work, carried out in a wilderness setting and accomplished principally by human and equine brawn. The man in the foreground in this image, holding the carpenter's square, appears to be Charles Arthur Stoess, the engineer in charge of the snowshed construction.

"Home" for the snowshed crews was a dormitory car, such as this one parked on siding track on the crest of Rogers Pass.

A completely engineered mountainside. A chain of snowsheds cloaked the line along Bear Creek at the eastern entrance to Rogers Pass. Detail in this remarkable view, taken between 1888 and 1890, shows firebreaks, diversion fences, and drainage ditching. The photographer, Norman Caple, paid his dues, lugging his large-format camera across the creek and onto the lower slopes of Mount Macdonald—and back again—to obtain this image.

water to the shed roofs. The longer sheds incorporated fire breaks into their construction.

Some of the snowsheds were on the valley floor, away from the mountainsides. Van Horne instructed Charles Arthur Stoess, the engineer in charge of the snowshed construction, to bury these "valley sheds" to strengthen them, effectively creating tunnels. Smoke from the locomotives would linger in the sheds, especially in the winter when snow would plug gaps in the cribbing, so the design engineers attempted to strike a balance between minimum length and maximum efficiency. Lastly, steam from the locomotives would condense on the shed ceilings in the winter, then drip to the rails and freeze, causing a loss of traction for the locomotives whose efficiency was already hampered by the steep grades near the pass.

When the CPR opened the Connaught Tunnel beneath Rogers Pass in 1916, it did not abandon all of its snowsheds. West of the pass, the railway crossed the Illecillewaet River ten times between Glacier and Revelstoke. Many of these crossings were made to dodge the worst side slopes and avalanche run outs, but sheds were still required at other locations. The greatest

Imagine the dismay of design engineers and snow-clearing crews when they were confronted with this scene in 1887. Note the distortion of the wall on the left, which is out of square due to the pressure of the snow. It is likely that this shed had to be rebuilt.

29 Shed was the first of three sheds for westbound trains on the north flank of the Illecillewaet Valley, between the second and third crossings of the Illecillewaet River on The Loops. This image, taken by A. B. Thom in the summer of 1887, shows a work camp adjacent to the structure. The tents would have been removed at the end of the season, but avalanches undoubtedly would have destroyed the cabins the following winter. Note the log bulwarks and cribbing above the shed, intended to direct avalanching snow. Mount Sir Donald (then known as Syndicate Peak) is in the background on the right, with Eagle Peak in the centre.

concentration of these, known as the Laurie Sheds, is still in use near Flat Creek, 13.3 miles west of Rogers Pass. In combination with a 513-foot rock tunnel and a 682-foot concrete tunnel, the thirteen adjoining snowsheds, now all made of concrete, cover 3,770 feet of track.

A tragic incident at the Laurie Sheds in 1937 epitomized the risk that avalanches posed to CPR employees. With the line blocked by a minor slide, a rotary plough crew, with one locomotive and two cabooses, steamed from Revelstoke to clear the obstruction. The men opened the track with relative ease and were preparing to head home when a second slide swept the track just ahead of the plough. The avalanche continued up the opposite side of the valley, where the debris stalled before toppling back into the valley bottom. It knocked the engine and cabooses into the Illecillewaet River. All escaped

The Stone Arch bridge at Cascade Creek. Cribbing and bulwarks at the western portal of 3 Shed are in the background.

except conductor Jack Macdonald, who was in the locomotive. As rescuers attempted to reach Macdonald, a third slide forced them back. A fourth avalanche then swept down to cover the locomotive with fifty feet of new debris. It took four days to recover Macdonald's body from the wreckage.

Sliding snow was not the only threat to the track in Rogers Pass. In late spring, debris flows from above the treeline would scour creek beds to the valley bottoms, where the muck plugged culverts and knocked out bridges. After one bridge had been demolished six times, the CPR hit upon the idea of hiring European stone masons to install stone arches that would carry the track over the offending streams. You can see one of these arches on the abandoned grade at Cascade Creek, about five miles east of Rogers Pass. Another of the stone masons' creations spanned the Illecillewaet River near Glacier House. You can admire this bridge from the 1885 Trail, which starts in the Illecillewaet campground.

☆ Fighting Back ☆

The world's first rotary snow plough was a Canadian solution to a very Canadian problem. Originally patented in 1869 by a Toronto dentist, the first prototype was built in Orangeville, Ontario, in 1883. Cooke Locomotive and Machine Works of New Jersey then developed rotary ploughs used on two US railroads in the winters of 1885-1886 and 1886-1887. Learning from this experience, in 1888, the CPR built eight rotary ploughs in cooperation with Poison Iron Works of Toronto. Each plough weighed 125,000 pounds, and had a cutting fan that was nine feet, 10.5 inches in diameter. The angle of the cutters was reversible, so an engineer could direct snow to either side of the track.

The rotaries eased the burden of clearing the heavy snowfalls and massive avalanche deposits in the mountains and in the Fraser Canyon. Prior to their introduction, the CPR had used wedge ploughs, but, as snow began to accumulate, these devices could not keep the track open without the assistance of shovelling gangs. Besides causing frequent and lengthy line closures, these clearing operations presented the CPR with the bother of finding a place to dump the cleared snow. The new rotaries, which were in effect giant snow blowers, solved the problem. When propelled by a single locomotive, a rotary could clear a three-foot-deep deposit of snow effortlessly. Deeper accumulations required an additional locomotive and the benefit of working downhill into the blockage. The engineer would move the plough forward and backward, biting away at the obstacle. In at least one case, with the assistance of shovellers who scooped material into the plough's path, a rotary was able to clear an avalanche deposit that was thirty-two feet deep.

At Rogers Pass, the CPR coupled rotary ploughs on either end of work locomotives in case, as often happened, a slide came down behind the train. When an avalanche deposit contained rock, ice, and timber, crews first used dynamite to break up the obstruction, a tactic that sometimes damaged the buried track. In 1911, the Montreal Locomotive Works delivered two monster rotary ploughs to the CPR. These each weighed 260,000 pounds and had an eleven-foot-diameter cutting fan. The CPR began retiring its rotary ploughs in 1940. By 1955, all were gone, replaced by wing ploughs and bulldozers.

Above: Wedge plough, locomotive with tender, and caboose at the second Rogers Pass station in the winter of 1886.

A rotary plough makes a final clean-up at the site of the 1910 avalanche in the crest of Rogers Pass. Note the terrace in the snow on the right. Shovelling gangs had excavated that amount of the cut by hand. One shovel remains on the terrace.

☆ On Time, Perhaps ☆

Pulled by locomotive 371, the first Pacific Express, the CPR's westbound passenger service, arrived precisely on time at Port Moody, BC, on July 4, 1886. It was the first train in western Canada to be scheduled according to the twenty-four-hour clock. Sandford Fleming's concept of standardized time (formerly called Greenwich Mean Time; now called Coordinated Universal Time) had been embraced by European and North American railroads in 1883. In the US, it was commonly known as "Railroad Time." Prior to 1883, each city set its clocks to noon when the sun reached its zenith. Thus, when it was noon in Montreal, it was 11:54 AM in Toronto, because Toronto is six minutes of longitude west of Montreal. Each railway chose a principal city on whose time it based its schedule. A passenger intent on catching a train in a different city had to know by how many minutes that city's clock differed from the railway's "home" city, and adjust the sprint to the ticket booth accordingly. Making successful connections between trains on competing railways required varying measures of providence and arithmetic.

Judging from the attending crowd, this photograph of CPR's Rotary Plough "C" at Rogers Pass was probably taken upon its delivery in 1888.

8

The White Death

Everyone who had ventured along the location line in Rogers Pass during the railway survey had been humbled by the steep slopes and the massive avalanche swaths through the forest. They reported avalanche deposits that plugged the valley bottoms until mid-August, and wondered what it would be like to see a slide come down. In the crossing of Rogers Pass alone, the CPR line cut through the runout zones of more than 130 avalanche paths. In many places, slides threatened the line from both sides of the valley. Wonder turned to fear on February 8, 1885, when three slides buried the location line just west of Rogers Pass, killing one man and injuring three. These were the first avalanche casualties attributed to what CPR workers soon called "the White Death."

Weather data from Glacier House (elevation 1,247 metres) at the turn of the twentieth century indicated an average annual snowfall of eleven metres, with snowfall recorded in all months except June, July, and August. The snowiest month was November, which averaged 2.4 metres of snow. January, February, and December were only slightly less snowy. Most summits adjacent to the CPR in Rogers Pass exceed 2,743 metres in elevation. Many of the avalanche paths are fed by slopes a mile high and more than a mile long. The snow at Rogers Pass is typically heavy due to its high water content: 801.4

Although Glacier House was not open for accommodation in the winter, the buildings required maintenance to protect them from collapse under the weight of the snow. Along with "harvesting" ice for the hotel's ice-house, snow clearing provided off-season work for the CPR's Swiss mountain guides.

kilograms per cubic metre. This arrangement of deep, heavy snow on steep slopes could only spell one thing—disaster.

The CPR required two railway sidings near the crest of the Selkirks: one, which it named Rogers Pass, to serve as a yard for trains and crews working the eastern approach in the Beaver Valley; the other, which it named Glacier, to serve west slope operations in the Illecillewaet Valley. The first Rogers Pass siding and station—a holdover from a construction camp—occupied the crest of the pass. Concerned about the potential for avalanches, and with train operations hampered by the opposing grades in either direction, the CPR relocated the station in 1887. The new station was two miles north on Bear Creek (now Connaught Creek), between 14 Shed and 15 Shed. The station house was situated at the convergence of two avalanche paths that descended from the slopes of Mount Rogers to the north, and from Mount Macdonald to the south.

In the winter of 1898–1899, 13.4 metres of snow fell at Rogers Pass. More than 2.7 metres of it came in January 1899. On the afternoon of January 30, an avalanche swept to the valley bottom from the slopes of Mount Macdonald, destroying the Rogers Pass station and yard, and killing eight of the ten people present, including the station master, his wife, and his two children. The woman was found with a rolling pin in one hand and pastry in the other. Although a great tragedy, it could have been worse; many other resident employees were away clearing another slide. Two railway superintendents should have been aboard a train in the yard at the time, but locomotive trouble had delayed their arrival.

The CPR moved the station again, this time one mile closer to the pass. After a decade with no avalanches at that location, the CPR diverted Bear Creek and rejigged the yard to improve the grades, building a fourth station. At the same time, it laid open track to bypass 17 Shed just south (railway-west) of the station.

In late February and early March 1910, the Selkirks were gripped by a storm that deposited two metres of snow at Rogers Pass in nine days. John Anderson, section foreman at the pass, later said it was the worst storm he had ever seen. None of his labourers spent a full night in bed for the duration, being continually summoned to deal with avalanches and drifting snow. On the afternoon of March 4, 1910, a slide came down from Cheops Mountain to the west of the track in the pass, launched off the abandoned 17 Shed, and buried six hundred feet of the new line. The CPR held eastbound and westbound passenger trains at nearby sidings and dispatched locomotive 1657 and sixty-two men, thirty-two of whom were Japanese, to assist a rotary plough in excavating the debris.

At 11:30 PM, watchman Joe Godfrey walked to his telephone shack in the Rogers Pass yard to advise the dispatcher in Revelstoke that the slide would be clear in a few hours. When Godfrey returned to the avalanche site, the plough, the locomotive, and all the men were missing, buried by another avalanche. This one had come down from Avalanche Mountain to the east, covering the same six hundred feet of track to a depth of thirty feet, burying most of the workers in the twenty-foot-deep cut they had just excavated, and killing one of the train crew. Only four people escaped. One of them was Bill LaChance, the fireman for locomotive 1657. LaChance had been sucked from the cab by the wind blast and had ridden within the avalanche, coming to rest atop the snow. When Godfrey found him, he asked, "Bill, where are they all?" LaChance, who had two badly broken legs, replied: "They're all gone."

Godfrey raced to the shack to call for help. The CPR always kept two locomotives at steam in Revelstoke, one pointed east, one pointed west. Bells and sirens sounded at midnight, calling one hundred volunteers to the station yard. After the men were hurriedly fed, they departed east on the rescue train. Another train came from Golden, picking up loggers and miners from camps along the way. Among those who came was photographer Byron Harmon,

☆ A Moving Target: Rogers Pass Station ☆

In the summer of 1885, Oliver Buell took this view of the construction camp at the summit of Rogers Pass, looking railway-east. Note the steep grade.

A year later, a booming "Summit City" occupied the same spot as that in the previous picture. The view is railway-west, opposite to the previous image.

Only a year later, "Summit City" was abandoned. Its derelict buildings remained a trackside feature for a decade. The view is railway-east.

This is perhaps the earliest photograph of the second Rogers Pass station, taken in 1887 by William Macfarlane Notman. The view is looking railway-east, with Mount Macdonald (then known as Mount Carroll) towering above the valley. Notman was standing adjacent to the siding track; the main line is in the background. The water tower is present; the station house is to its left (east), with the roundhouse to the left, across the main line from the station house. In later photographs the station house is west of the water tower. The entrance to 15 Shed would have been just to the photographer's right. (see map on p. 30 for station locations.)

The threat should have been obvious; nonetheless, the second Rogers Pass station bordered the runout zone of a massive avalanche path from Mount Macdonald—evidenced by the tangle of downed trees behind the station house. The 40,000-gallon water tower is the cylindrical building, right of centre, partially obscured by a tree. The two-stall roundhouse is to the right of the water tower; the roof of 15 Shed—protruding from the downed trees—is in the distance, just to the left of the water tower.

The Rogers Pass snow removal gang—most of whom were Finlanders—posing on the platform of the original station house at the second Rogers Pass station, ca. 1890.

Little remained of the Rogers Pass roundhouse following the 1899 avalanche.

The third Rogers Pass station occupied a landscape of stumps and spars, albeit with a magnificent backdrop. This view is looking railway-east into the dead-end yard, with Mount Tupper in the background. The five-stall roundhouse is the low, dark building on siding track, left of centre. The seventy-foot turntable is aligned with the open door of the right-hand stall, toward which a locomotive is under steam. The water tower is the cylindrical building, lower right. It had a spout on either side so that it could water trains on the main line or on siding track. The main line (on a 1.6 percent grade) curves to the right to pass between the water tower and the station house, where a small crowd awaits a train. Photographer R. H. Trueman would have had his back to the north portal of 16 Shed. Compare details in this image with the one on p. iii taken in the same era, before the CPR made a grade revision here in 1909.

who would record haunting images of the grisly scene. The rescuers from the east had to walk the last three miles to the accident because another slide had plugged the valley at the site of the second Rogers Pass station.

In the light of morning, the scale of the tragedy became apparent. The avalanche had ripped the locomotive and the rotary plough apart and had flung the sixty-two-ton plough onto the roof of the snowshed, forty feet above and sixty feet away from the line. More than five hundred feet of the snowshed was "splintered like match wood." Because there were bodies in the snow, much of the deposit had to be shovelled by hand. Six hundred men took part. All of the Japanese labourers had been killed. Rescuers found many of the dead still standing. One group of three faced each other, caught in midconversation. One of the men held a pipe in his hand. Foreman John Anderson's younger brother was among the dead. The youngest killed was twenty, the oldest, fifty. The town of Revelstoke was in mourning for two weeks, with funerals often numbering three per day.

This tragedy—variously reported as resulting in either fifty-eight or sixty-two dead—as of 2009, remains the greatest loss of life in a single avalanche in Canada. (Four of the bodies were not recovered until the spring thaw. The CPR had included these in the original death toll of fifty-eight, but later writers added the four to create a false total of sixty-two.)

Within a week, an inquest into the avalanche convened at Golden to address two questions. First, by paying workers time-and-a-half to work at night, was the CPR enticing men to carry out unnecessarily dangerous work?

The north portal of 18 Shed is in the background of this view, which shows rescuers clearing the deposit of the 1910 avalanche.

☆ Three Times Lucky ☆

A few days after the March 4, 1910, avalanche, watchman Joe Godfrey dug patrolman Adrian Lathbury out from another slide. Lathbury lived with his dog in a trackside shack built from salvaged snowshed timbers. Godfrey had been prompted to look for Lathbury when he found the dog alone, digging in the slide. Godfrey later recounted that Lathbury was "proof against something." A few years earlier, the patrolman had fallen off a trestle into a swamp and had been dragged out alive. A year after that he had fallen off a freight train and had an arm amputated as a result of his injuries. The CPR gave him the patrolman's job to keep him out of trouble and on the payroll. Lathbury's dog was later buried in another avalanche and was also dug out alive.

Second, did the failure to post lookouts at the avalanche site constitute negligence? The inquest failed to return a verdict; however, a second inquest found no blame and returned a verdict of "accidental death." The jury noted the slide path was one for which there had been no prior record of avalanches, and that the weather that had contributed to the slide had been extraordinary—four days earlier, ninety-six people had died in an avalanche when rain fell on snow at Stevens Pass, Washington, on the Great Northern Railway. The jury recommended that the CPR "withdraw their workmen from service at all slides in future during stormy nights." (The CPR failed to comply with this recommendation.) The inquest was completed just twelve days after the avalanche, with evidence given in a single morning and the jury returning the verdict before lunch after forty-five minutes of deliberation.

Although it may seem a logical consequence of the 1910 avalanche, the CPR did not build the Connaught Tunnel beneath Rogers Pass because of it. The company had been contemplating the tunnel since 1906, and had been surveying alternate routes that would have avoided Rogers Pass. Even after the tunnel was completed, avalanches, and the rockslides they sometimes released, continued to kill CPR workers on the approaches to the pass. These accidents usually involved trains colliding with avalanche debris, or were derailments caused by track damaged by avalanches. In all, some 250 CPR workers have been killed in avalanche-related accidents near Rogers Pass. The communities of Revelstoke and Golden, where many of these workers lived, long ago learned to abide with this unsettling reality of mountain railroading.

9

The House
at the Pass

For the first twenty-four years of its mountain operations, the CPR did not add dining cars to its trains. The railway owned few dining cars at the time, and adding one in the mountains would have required an additional helper locomotive, each of which cost $12,000 per year to operate. Instead, William Cornelius Van Horne directed that dining cars be parked at three sidings: North Bend in the Fraser Canyon, Glacier station in Rogers Pass, and Field at the western base of Kicking Horse Pass; and that trains be scheduled to arrive at meal times.

The scenery overshadowed the cuisine at all three mountain dining stops. Many of the guests wanted to stay and explore. By late October 1886, the CPR had replaced the dining car at Field with a building that included a few rooms for overnight guests, creating Mount Stephen House—the railway's first mountain hotel. Work on the original Glacier House at Rogers Pass also began that year, with the hotel opening in December. Located on what was then known as Glacier Creek, just south of the pass, it included a dining hall and fifteen bedrooms, half of which were used by staff. Under the terms of an elaborate contract, Harry Perley managed Glacier House for the CPR to provide "a strictly first-class Hotel Dining Station in the very best style." By all accounts, Perley succeeded.

The Ille-Cille-Wait Hotel—just west of the future site of Glacier House—typified trackside accommodation during construction of the CPR. Among its enticements, Ed Lawler's establishment offered "choice liquors and cigars" and, evidently, harp music. If William Cornelius Van Horne had not directed the creation of the CPR's mountain hotels, this kind of accommodation may have prevailed, trackside and elsewhere.

In 1899, the CPR brought three Swiss guides to Glacier House: Edward Feuz (pronounced Foits) Sr., Christian Häsler Sr., and Charlie Clarke, a Swiss with an English name. Feuz and Häsler established the profession of mountain guiding in Canada when they led the first ascent of Mount Dawson on August 13 of that same year. The following year, the CPR brought guides to Mount Stephen House at Field, and, two years later, to the chalet at Lake Louise, where the railway company's guiding operation would enjoy its greatest longevity.

The railway undertook two major expansions at Glacier House. The first, completed in 1892 at a cost of just under $20,000, added thirty-two bedrooms and a bowling alley to the hotel. Fountains, laundry shacks, and outbuildings came and went as the railway added servants' quarters, a billiard room, and a lunch room by 1897. The second expansion, known as "the Wing," contained fifty-four rooms with elevator service. The Wing cost $32,600 and opened in 1904. By that time, Glacier station and Glacier House comprised a rambling string of six buildings that stretched southward from the railway track. With its backdrop of spectacular peaks and glacial ice, it was a destination unique in North America.

With Mount Sir Donald as the principal drawing card, Glacier House soon became the centre of alpinism in North America. Although climbs of

The station house (right) and the hotel were under construction at Glacier in this view in the autumn of 1886, probably taken by government surveyor, Otto Klotz.

Three years later, the original building had acquired its first addition, and the grounds had sprouted a fountain. However, the grooming ended a short distance to the south in a field of stumps. This clearing would later be the site of "The Wing." (see photos on p. 121). The photograph was taken October 7, 1889.

Cool summer fun: Christian Häsler Sr. led this rope of novices on the Illecillewaet Glacier in 1900—close to comforts and peril.

the 1890s are better known as having taken place in the Rockies, most of the celebrated alpinists who visited the Rockies also stopped at Glacier House. The hotel became so popular, climbers out on routes for several days would return to find their rooms rented out again, and their spare camping equipment unpacked by manager Perley and pitched on the lawn to accommodate others. The CPR parked a dormitory car at the adjacent siding so as not to turn away customers.

The demise of Glacier House was slow but inevitable. With greater locomotive power available, the CPR began to add dining cars to its trains in 1909, eliminating the need for scheduled stops at mealtimes. Also the Illecillewaet Glacier—the principal attraction for casual visitors—was receding rapidly. By 1925, its terminus had gone back so far (689 metres from where it had first been measured) that it was no longer visible from the hotel grounds. With the opening of the Connaught Tunnel in 1916, the CPR moved Glacier station 1.5 miles west to the west portal of the tunnel. Glacier House remained open, with guests delivered along a wagon road by horse-drawn carriages or by sleds. After the wooden wing of the Chateau Lake Louise burned in 1924, the CPR—fearing the same for Glacier House—closed it. The railway

At its peak, Glacier House presented a bizarre yet alluring combination of structures and styles.

The lobby of Glacier House was evidently a gentleman's paradise during its heyday.

drew plans for a stone-built expansion in 1926 but never broke ground for the project. For a few years, hardy travellers hiked along the wagon road and roughed it in the vacant buildings. Demolition took place in the summer and autumn of 1929, with most of the rubbish burned and the site left relatively undisturbed. The CPR shipped much of the furniture from Glacier House to the Chateau Lake Louise, but many artifacts made their way to dwellings in Revelstoke.

Some mountaineers continued to use the site of Glacier House as a campground; others stayed nearby in an old railway maintenance building known as the Red Barn. Formal accommodation came to Rogers Pass again when the Alpine Club of Canada built the Wheeler Hut in 1947. Archaeologists inventoried the grounds of Glacier House between 1984 and 1986. Today, the location is a National Historic Site (separate from the Rogers Pass National Historic Site), reached by an easy walk on the 1885 Trail from Illecillewaet campground.

The Vaux family took many photographs of the Great Glacier (Illecillewaet Glacier), but the earliest large-format photograph is this one, taken by William Macfarlane Notman in 1887. It shows the glacier within a few decades of when it had begun to recede from its "Little Ice Age" maximum size.

☆ Home for the Summer ☆

Members of the Vaux (pronounced Vox) family of Philadelphia were among the celebrated visitors to Glacier House. In July 1887, George Vaux Sr. and his three children—George Jr., Mary, and William—made whistle stops in the mountains of western Canada. On their next trip in 1894, the family noted how much the toe of the Illecillewaet Glacier had melted back. With an interest in glaciers awakened, the Vauxes returned to Glacier House in 1897 and 1898, and took numerous photographs and measurements. This information allowed the brothers to write the first treatise on North American mountain ice.

The Vauxes were not pretending to be experts. Glaciology, as we know it today, did not then exist. The theory of ice ages was relatively new, and the geologists who held domain over rocks and ice still disputed what constituted evidence of the earth's glacial past. Little was known of the Rockies and Selkirks beyond what could be seen from the railway grade. Certainly, no one was studying glaciers. Into this *terra incognita*, the Vauxes brought their curiosity, their cameras, their exuberance, and their mantra that epitomized the late-Victorian era: "[S]o little exploration has been carried out that each visitor is practically a new discoverer."

The Vauxes' principal contribution to future glaciology was the application of photography to recording glacial change. Between 1898 and 1912, various members of the family returned to the Rockies and Selkirks eleven times. Their journals record them riding the rails as they hopscotched between Banff, Lake Louise, Field, and Glacier House. When they reached their subject glaciers, the Vauxes would set up their equipment on the same vantage points, align their cameras carefully along compass bearings, and take what they called "test photographs" of the same scenes year after year. This process, known today as repeat photography, provided a time-lapse record of landscape change.

The Vauxes were passionate artists, but with a modesty that called attention to the subject matter, not themselves. Their work bridged the chasm between the drawing rooms of eastern North America and the alien, western landscapes of serac and moraine. It was a Vaux family trademark for William and George Jr. to place people in their glacier compositions. How many train tickets the CPR sold, and how many rooms it booked at its chain of mountain hotels as a result of this subtle promotion will never be known. Certainly, the Vaux family raised a collective curiosity, transforming at least part of the North American population into a rank of budding naturalists and mountaineers.

☆ Two Giants, Two Tragedies ☆

On September 2, 1858, geologist James Hector's party from the Palliser Expedition made the first recorded crossing of Kicking Horse Pass in the Rockies, travelling from west to east. Four days earlier, near Wapta Falls, in present-day BC, Hector had been kicked in the chest by a horse. According to Hector's later recollection, the impact had rendered him unconscious for so long that his companions had dug a grave for him by the time he had revived.

Following the Palliser Expedition, Hector became director of the Geological Survey and Colonial Museum of New Zealand. In August 1903, Hector returned to Canada for the first time since 1859 with his son Douglas. Among the senior Hector's objectives were to revisit Wapta Falls to see if he could find his "grave," and to cross Kicking Horse Pass by train.

At Glacier House on the evening of August 14, Douglas became unwell. Although James Hector had been trained as a medical doctor, he did not act on his son's discomfort and another doctor's recommendation that Douglas be taken to Revelstoke hospital immediately. When it became apparent to Hector that Douglas was truly ill, the pair boarded a freight train in the night. Douglas, suffering from appendicitis, had emergency surgery in Revelstoke but died later that day from the infection. Hector telegraphed the news to Glacier House, from where a small contingent headed to Revelstoke on August 16 for the funeral. Among those who came was Edward Whymper, "conqueror of the Matterhorn," the tragic figure who, in 1865, had survived the descent of that mountain during which four of his companions had fallen to their deaths. So, two giants of exploration met in the wilds of western Canada and, by the fortuitous presence of a camera-toting Mary Schäffer, were photographed together at the funeral service. Hector abandoned his plans and sailed for New Zealand later that week, never to return to Canada. His health soon failed and he died in 1907.

Above: James Hector (seated) and Edward Whymper.

☆ Mountain Man ☆

Following the creation of Glacier National Park in 1886 and the rise of alpinism at Glacier House in the 1890s, the Canadian government decided to map the area to help promote it to tourists. In 1901-1902, the federal Department of the Interior assigned the task to a team headed by Dominion Land Surveyor Arthur Oliver Wheeler. At the time, Wheeler had been a surveyor for twenty years, with more than a decade of experience in the mountains of western Canada. In the course of mapping the Selkirk Mountains, Wheeler truly became an accom-

plished mountaineer. In 1905, the results of his labours appeared in a two-volume book, *The Selkirk Range*. From 1903 to 1910, Wheeler mapped the main range of the Rockies. In 1907, he helped found the Alpine Club of Canada—making good on an idea that Sandford Fleming had first floated when crossing Rogers Pass in 1883. Wheeler served as the club's first president for four years, and spent another seventeen years on the executive. In 1911, he led an expedition to explore the Mount Robson region, which led to the creation of Mount Robson Provincial Park. From 1913 to 1925, Wheeler was British Columbia's commissioner on the Interprovincial Boundary Survey with Alberta. It can safely be said that by the end of that survey, Wheeler had seen more of the mountains of western Canada, and had climbed more of them, than any other person alive. His maps, made using a technique called photo-topography, today stand as works of art.

Despite, or perhaps as a result of his accomplishments, many of Wheeler's contemporaries found him to be autocratic and arrogant. He named a fine peak in the Selkirks after himself—no other Canadian surveyor has ever done likewise. The photograph above appeared in the 1913 *Canadian Alpine Journal* with the caption: "He who must be obeyed." Wheeler's first wife was Clara Macoun, daughter of the eminent Canadian botanist, John Macoun. Their son, Edward Oliver Wheeler, grew to be an accomplished mountaineer, and became Surveyor General of India.

Above: Arthur Oliver Wheeler.

☆ A Timely Fashion ☆

If coveralls and a distinctive cap were the signatures of a locomotive engineer in the days of steam, the pocket watch on a chain was synonymous with the conductor. It was the conductor who ran the show; no train raised steam to pull out of a station until the conductor gave the nod. On the single-tracked railways of the late nineteenth century, that nod was governed by time. North American railways adopted standards for pocket watches in 1891 following a disaster at Kipton, Ohio, when a conductor's watch that had stopped for four minutes and then restarted caused a collision between two trains in which nine people died.

Every member of a train crew—the engineer, fireman, brakemen, conductor—supplied his own watch. It was customary for the crew to compare timepieces at the beginning of a run. Railroaders bought the best watches they could afford. Those with twenty-three-jewel movements were standard; seventeen-jewel movements were the minimum allowed. Arabic numerals were preferred on the watch face, which had to be white. Most watches had each minute indicated, with every fifth minute highlighted in red. The CPR mandated that a conductor's pocket watch be accurate to within thirty seconds per week. Each pocket watch was checked every two weeks by a jeweller under contract to the railway. Conductors carried a maintenance card that logged these inspections and any resulting calibrations.

The photographer's private car awaits Oliver Buell on the Mountain Creek bridge, soon after its completion in 1885.

10

Down Under

The Connaught Tunnel

The propelling force of gravity and the crushing weight of snow have twice forced the CPR underground to improve operations at Rogers Pass. William Cornelius Van Horne's initial plan had been to double-track the pass to simplify scheduling, given the considerable delays caused by adding and removing helper locomotives. However, after a few seasons of experience with avalanches it was clear that the cost of building and maintaining double-track snowsheds would not be money well spent. A tunnel was needed to protect the track from avalanches while reducing the grade.

Although Van Horne may have dreamed of a tunnel under Rogers Pass as early as 1888, he knew the CPR could ill afford the enterprise. So, as it had done on the Big Hill east of Field, the railway, at great human cost, toughed it out for twenty-five years until the money became available. The commitment to build the tunnel marked a transition in the economic rationale of the CPR, from low capital cost/high maintenance to the opposite—a principle that endures today.

When the Rogers Pass Tunnel construction tender went out early in 1913, the CPR advised contractors that, "Everything else being equal, the party who will guarantee completion in the shortest time will be the one who will receive the work." The firm of Foley, Welch and Stewart, which had just built much of the Grand Trunk Pacific Railway west of Edmonton, continued its dominance of Canadian railway construction when it secured the contract on July 1, 1913.

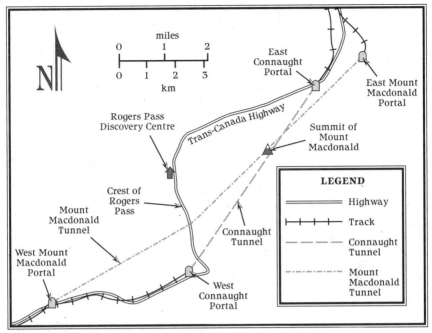

Rogers Pass, showing the alignments of the Connaught Tunnel and the Mount Macdonald Tunnel. The original railway grade roughly paralleled the route of today's Trans-Canada Highway.

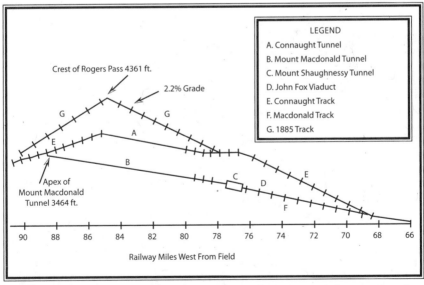

Elevation view comparing the original railway grade, the Connaught Tunnel, and the Rogers Pass Project.

Compressed air supplied the bulk of the power, but human courage was no small detail during the excavation of the main heading in the Connaught Tunnel.

A tale of two tunnels: Tunnelling technology changed greatly in the 70 years between construction of the Connaught Tunnel (top and centre) and the Mount Macdonald Tunnel (bottom). The auxiliary tunnel is on the left in the top view. In the view of the Mount Macdonald Tunnel (looking railway-east), the main tunnel is on the left; the right-hand tunnel connects to the central ventilation shaft.

The contractor proposed an unusual tunnelling method for the project. Instead of excavating a pioneer heading that would subsequently be widened, crews would build two tunnels. An auxiliary tunnel, eight feet by eight feet in dimension, would be driven first, about fifty feet away from, and ten feet above, the alignment of the principal tunnel. The auxiliary tunnel would carry compressed air, ventilation, water, and track for bringing in equipment and for removing spoil. From the auxiliary tunnel, crews would bore across to the alignment of the main tunnel. From the end of each of these crosscuts, the main tunnel, initially eleven feet wide and nine feet high, would be advanced in two directions. The CPR agreed to the plan. Twelve such crosscuts were eventually made.

Before any tunnelling could begin, Foley, Welch and Stewart had to build 4.5 miles of temporary track on steep sidehills to reach the portals. The company erected construction communities at each portal and at Glacier station. Collectively, the settlements housed the five hundred workers required for the project. West of the tunnel, crews had to divert a nine-hundred-foot-long section of the Illecillewaet River to protect the grade from flooding.

Work began on April 2, 1914. The principal tools employed were dynamite, hammer drills, and steam shovels powered by compressed air. Crews timbered the tunnels as they advanced, and used "light cars" of 0.5 cubic yard capacity to haul away the spoil. These dump trains were sometimes hauled by hand or by mules, then by locomotives powered by compressed air, and later by a gasoline-fuelled minilocomotive. The CPR agreed to pay its workers a bonus based on footage excavated per month, pro-rated to the amount of solid rock involved. With crews thus inspired and working three eight-hour shifts each day, it took just sixteen months to complete 19,610 feet of auxiliary tunnel. As the excavation and enlargement of the main tunnel had taken place simultaneously, only another seven months were required to finish the work.

Connecting the two portals came in December 1915, with an error of alignment of less than six inches. In its final dimensions, the main tunnel was twenty-nine feet wide and twenty-four feet high. There were escape bays every quarter-mile and telephones every half-mile. Tunnelling at the west end proved easier than at the east end because there was less water in the cut and more stable terrain. The west end crews were able to average about 25 percent more distance per day.

Workers called the main tunnel "the big hole." They poured 500,000 sacks of cement into its concrete lining, which they formed in twenty-two-foot sections, each of which took five days to clear, pour, and set. More than one hundred high-powered electric lamps illuminated the work. Cooks fed workers on the job at restaurants in the auxiliary tunnel, accessed by doors from the main tunnel.

Crews diverted the Illecillewaet River at the west end of the Connaught Tunnel before construction began, but on September 5, 1931, the river surged over the berm and plugged four hundred feet of the tunnel and 1,500 feet of the cutting to the west with boulders and debris. It took five days for workers to reopen the track.

The finished main tunnel was 5.022 miles long, and, apart from slight curves near each portal, climbed in a straight line on a grade of 0.98 percent. When standing fifty feet inside a portal during daytime, a worker could see a pinpoint of light from the other portal. The tunnel passed through Mount Macdonald 5,690 feet beneath its summit. It was the longest railway tunnel in North America until it was eclipsed in 1928 by the 6.21-mile-long Moffat Tunnel in Colorado. When Arthur William Patrick Albert—the Duke of Connaught, Canada's Governor-General, and Queen Victoria's third son— visited on July 18, 1916, he named the tunnel the Selkirk Tunnel. Within a few weeks, the CPR renamed it in the Duke's honour, and also renamed Bear Creek, at the eastern entry to Rogers Pass, Connaught Creek.

The Connaught Tunnel reduced the length of the CPR main line by 4.4 miles. Gone were more than four miles of snowsheds and the looping alignment west of Rogers Pass equivalent to seven full circles. The apex of the climb in the tunnel was 552 feet lower than the crest of the original railway grade, and came approximately five hundred feet from the tunnel's west portal. Completion of the tunnel was a tremendous achievement but went almost unnoticed against the backdrop of World War I, which had greatly complicated the effort due to shortages of steel and labour, and an increase in the price of dynamite.

As with all of the CPR's major construction projects, the Connaught Tunnel's transition from drawing board to reality came with unforeseen headaches and costs. The CPR had assumed that, because of the tunnel's length and the resulting difficulty of providing fresh air, train operations would have to be electrified. When the planned electrification proved too costly, the CPR built a diesel-powered ventilation facility at the west portal to remove train exhaust. Two five-hundred-horsepower motors drove a pair of thirteen-foot-diameter fans. After tunnel operations began on December 9, 1916, it was found that the ventilation was inadequate. Westbound trains frequently stalled. Crews were issued gas masks. The CPR reworked the ventilation system and assigned oil-fuelled locomotives, just then being introduced, to tunnel service because they were cleaner burning than coal-fired locomotives. In normal double-track operations, locomotives ran forward on the right-hand track. In the Connaught Tunnel, the CPR ran trains forward on the left-hand track in order to place the engineer's window closer to the centre of the track to improve visibility.

Rockfalls plagued the tunnel, and icy rails caused westbound locomotives to stall because of poor traction. In the early 1920s, the CPR lined the tunnel with reinforced concrete to eliminate rockfall and reduce water seeps. The tunnel is still in use today. Because the eastern approach is still ruled by the lengthy 2.2 percent grade on the climb from Rogers siding, the tunnel generally carries eastbound trains, many of which consist of empty hopper cars.

The Connaught Tunnel cost $5.5 million to build, of which the CPR spent $2.5 million on dynamite. The attendant above-ground track revisions totalled 10.4 miles and cost another $3 million. The CPR ran double-track in the tunnel until November 11, 1958, when the advent of container cars and double-decked automobile carriers necessitated a single track on the centre line to provide the required headroom.

In July 1917, the CPR abandoned the above-ground line over Rogers Pass. A labour shortage hampered the salvage operations, but by October, eighteen miles of track and twenty-five thousand feet of snowsheds had been torn up. Crews salvaged the bridges the following summer. Some of the snowshed cribbing was so well entrenched, the CPR decided against removing it. Much of that cribbing and the bridge masonry work endures almost a century after it last received maintenance. With completion of the bridge removal in 1918, the crest of Rogers Pass was free from most human intrusion until the construction of the Trans-Canada Highway in the late 1950s.

☆ The Mountain Locomotive ☆

The steep grades between Calgary and Revelstoke taxed the efficiency and safety of the CPR's mountain operations. In July 1929, the railway introduced the first of twenty units of a much-hoped-for solution: Class T1a, a series of massive locomotives with a 2-10-4 wheel configuration (two "pony" wheels, ten driving wheels, and four driving wheels under the tender), and numbered in sequence beginning with 5900. Built by the Locomotive and Machine Company of Montreal (later called the Montreal Locomotive Works), this locomotive-type was eventually named the "Selkirk" as a result of a competition among CPR employees.

The Selkirk became the pinnacle of Canadian motive power in the steam era. Its ten driving wheels were each five feet, three inches in diameter. The four trailing wheels were coupled to an auxiliary engine, used to assist the unit at speeds up to twelve miles per hour. Weighing 365 tons and measuring just inches shy of 100 feet long, a fully loaded Selkirk carried 4,100 gallons of bunker-C fuel oil, and 12,000 gallons of water. It consumed about forty gallons of oil and eighty-eight gallons of water for each mile travelled in the mountains. Two sand domes atop the engine housing held material for sanding the rails to increase traction.

On a flat grade, a single Selkirk could haul 2,850 tons—equivalent to forty-five passenger cars. Four Selkirks were required to pull a four-thousand-ton freight train up the Hill east of Revelstoke. A single Selkirk could manage a sixteen-car, one-thousand-ton passenger train from Calgary to Revelstoke. Individual Selkirks were dedicated as helpers based at Field or Revelstoke, or as road locomotives based at Calgary or Revelstoke. (The run for a Selkirk-powered passenger train from Revelstoke to Calgary required about twelve hours and a crew change at Field, the division point between the CPR's Laggan and Mountain subdivisions.)

The CPR introduced the second series of Selkirks, Class T1b (numbered 5920-5929), beginning in November 1938. These had a more streamlined look. The railway deployed the last six Selkirks, Class T1c (numbered 5930-5935), beginning in February 1949. The CPR removed the Selkirks from mountain service in 1952, replacing them with diesel-electric locomotives. Some Selkirks saw use on the prairies until 1959, by which time most had been scrapped, despite still having years of potential working life. Only two Selkirk T1c locomotives escaped the cutting torch: 5931 is at Heritage Park in Calgary; and 5935 is at the Canadian Railway Museum in Delson-Saint Constant, Quebec.

Selkirk-type, Class T1b, locomotive 5923, under steam on The Hill east of Revelstoke. Note the secondary plume, indicating that the auxiliary engine was in use.

A fireman's-eye view of the interior of a Selkirk locomotive cab, with the brakeman (left) and the engineer.

☆ Tinkering with a Good Idea ☆

The Selkirk-type locomotive proved ideal for mountain service. Hoping to improve on the idea, the CPR's locomotive chief, Henry Blaine Bowen, designed an experimental locomotive with the same 2-10-4 wheel configuration as the Selkirk but employing a complex system of multiple boilers. Known as the Class T4a, the CPR numbered the locomotive 8000. It first raised steam at the company's Angus Shops in Montreal on May 29, 1931. Multipressure locomotives were also developed at about the same time in the US and Europe, but, with a length of 99 feet, 3 inches, and weighing 795,300 pounds with a fully loaded tender, the T4a was by far the largest and most complex steam locomotive ever built. Its engine had three boilers whose collective steam drove three pistons, and its driving wheels were sixty-three inches in diameter. Its massive tender held twelve thousand gallons of water and 4,100 gallons of fuel oil.

In theory, the T4a was powerful enough to single-handedly haul a train of 150 forty-ton freight cars in the mountains. The CPR assigned it to the run between Revelstoke and Field, and was obliged to beef up the rails to take its pounding. The T4a developed 1,350 pounds per square inch of pressure. Train men considered it a bomb waiting to go off and found any excuse not to crew it. Not surprisingly, the T4a was a high-maintenance item. Although it used 15 percent less fuel than a Selkirk in the mountains, the T4a locomotive spent 30 percent of its working life under repair at the CPR's Ogden Shops in Calgary—including one eleven-month stretch. The CPR took the T4a out of service in September 1936 after it had run 50,410 miles. The following month, it was taken to Montreal, where it was scrapped in 1940. The CPR salvaged its tender and snow plough.

Locomotive 8000 on siding track just west of the Connaught Tunnel.

The Rogers Pass Project

Between 1965 and 1980, freight carried by CP Rail across Rogers Pass quadrupled. Freight traffic forecasts indicated that the line would reach its maximum capacity by the mid-1980s. The 2.2 percent grade east of the pass dictated that six helper locomotives be cut into each long, westbound train. The resulting delay—as much as two and one-half hours—restricted traffic to fifteen trains in each direction daily. At three other locations in western Canada, where it ran loaded trains on grades of more than 1 percent (Notch Hill, Clanwilliam, and Stephen), CP Rail spent $46 million in the late 1970s and early 1980s to reduce those grades and eliminate the need for helper locomotives. Despite the implementation of the Centralized Traffic Control System in the late 1950s to coordinate train movements, the eastern approach to Rogers Pass remained the single greatest impediment to efficiency on CP Rail's main line.

After toying with electrification of the line in the 1970s (CP Rail installed a test section of track near Ross Peak siding, west of Rogers Pass), and with various routings of the line in the Beaver Valley (one of which would have included two spiral tunnels), on July 31, 1981, CP Rail proposed the Rogers Pass Project. This $550 million solution was 21.6 miles long and consisted of six elements: the 9.11-mile-long Mount Macdonald Tunnel; the 1.14-mile-long Mount Shaughnessy Tunnel; the 4,032-foot-long John Fox Viaduct; six bridges; a new siding; and grade modifications to the existing track, which included turning old sidings into sections of double-track. The new routing, with a grade of less than 1 percent and intended predominantly for westbound traffic, was designated the Macdonald Track. The old routing became known as the Connaught Track.

The Rogers Pass Project eventually employed one thousand workers. Work on the double-tracking began with the construction of a bridge to carry the new track over Cupola Creek at mile 68.2 (as measured west from Field). From this point, the relative elevations of the two tracks diverged rapidly, at an average of sixty-three feet per mile. The crest of the climb on the Macdonald Track came west of Rogers Pass at precisely the western portal of the Macdonald Tunnel at an elevation of 3,464 feet.

The project was replete with engineering challenges, but because the Macdonald Track crossed tributary streams much lower down on the mountainsides, the bridges required, although sometimes longer than those on the Connaught Track, were not as imposing. Mountain Creek was spanned by two trestles totalling 315 feet. Seven steel spans, totalling seven hundred feet, bridged Stoney Creek. A culvert sufficed to span Surprise Creek. Where the alignments of the tunnels cross, just northeast of the summit of Mount Macdonald, the Mount Macdonald Tunnel is 298.6 feet beneath the Connaught

Tunnel and 849.8 feet lower than the crest of Rogers Pass. The only connection between the two tunnels is a test bore made in 1979 as part of a geologic survey to determine the feasibility of the Mount Macdonald Tunnel.

The interior of the tunnel is lined with unreinforced concrete, which, besides providing strength, reduces the resistance of airflow and hence improves tunnel ventilation. The horseshoe-shaped tunnel is twenty-five feet, ten inches high, and is seventeen feet wide on straight track and eighteen feet wide on curves. It is lit from end to end and is large enough to permit

This aerial view of the Beaver River valley, looking south, shows the Connaught Track on the right, with the grade for the new Macdonald Track on the left.

In this aerial view of Rogers Pass the massive concrete housing that covers the west portal of the Macdonald Tunnel, pokes above ground between the Trans-Canada Highway and the Connaught Track (see p. 108 for a close-up view.) The Macdonald and Connaught tracks merge just beyond the right-hand edge of the photograph. Mount Sir Donald is in the background; the Illecillewaet River is on the right.

The central ventilation shaft for the Mount Macdonald Tunnel is 1,145 feet deep, with a diameter of 28 feet. It took 22 months to blast and drill.

future electrification. The rail bed does not use ties, ballast, or spikes. The rails are attached with clips to a continuous, nine-inch-thick concrete slab known as PACT-track. After installing PACT-track on a section of the main line near Albert Canyon in 1984, CP Rail chose to use it in the tunnel to eliminate the line closures and the costs associated with tie replacement.

The Mount Macdonald Tunnel is the twenty-fifth longest railway tunnel in the world, and is by far the longest in the Americas. (The next longest is the 7.79-mile Seattle-St. Paul Tunnel on the Great Northern Railway.) Given the tunnel's length, design engineers knew that artificial ventilation would be required to prevent the buildup of heat and fumes that would cause locomotives to stall. The system would also be required to purge the tunnel of fumes so that trains could use the tunnel in rapid succession. The tunnel is effectively split in half at the midpoint, with electrically powered doors at

☆ A Boring Job ☆

Two contractors excavated the Mount Macdonald Tunnel under separate contracts and by using different techniques. From the east portal, most of the work was carried out by a sophisticated device, the Tunnel Boring Machine. Nicknamed "the Mole," the electrically powered machine was twenty-two feet in diameter and weighed three hundred tons. Its various components were shipped to Rogers Pass on twenty railway cars. Assembly of the machine took more than six weeks. The Mole moved on its own track, its fifty-two cutting discs taking a massive circular bite out of the alignment. The Mole averaged seventy-five feet of excavation per day, and on one day managed 206 feet—a world record for tunneling at this diameter in solid rock. After the Mole completed the tunnel opening from the east, the remainder of the excavation was carried out by drilling and blasting. From the west portal, the tunnelling was a more conventional attack on the full dimension of the cutting face, using a massive electric drill and blasting. A huge shovel cleared the debris. Construction from the east portal began on August 27, 1984, and from the west on October 5. Connection of the two portals occurred on October 24, 1986.

The Tunnel Boring Machine excavated the eastern section of the Mount Macdonald Tunnel.

the east portal and at the centre. There is a backup door at each location that can be engaged should a primary door fail to close. If the doors lose power, they automatically spring open so trains will not collide with them. As a second fail-safe, the doors are made of wood, with panels designed to break should a train hit them. The doors retract vertically and are decked with reflective stripes. Sirens sound when the doors begin to move.

Shafts for fresh air and exhaust air, and two fan houses are also part of the system. Four fans are located in the fan house atop the central shaft. A fifth fan is at the east portal. Each fan is driven by a 2,250 horsepower motor. A backup diesel generator supplies power in the event of an electrical outage. Sensors monitor the air quality in the tunnel, feeding the information to a computer that controls the mix of exhaust air and fresh air necessary to maintain operating conditions for the locomotives. The computer is programmed with a multitude of modes to create the optimal conditions for different complements of trains, and for the requirements of westbound and eastbound travel. Controls for the computer are located at the Revelstoke yard, and in the ventilation building adjacent to the east portal. Operators can override the computer or choose semi-automatic operations, tailoring the air mix to tunnel conditions. It takes about thirty minutes for a westbound train to negotiate the tunnel. Under optimum conditions, another westbound train can enter the tunnel ten minutes later.

The Rogers Pass Project also included construction of the 1.14-mile-long Mount Shaughnessy Tunnel, located 4,386 feet east of the Mount Macdonald Tunnel. The Mount Shaughnessy Tunnel was driven in a single heading from the west. Excavation spoil was used to fill the grade between the two tunnels. The rail bed in the Mount Shaughnessy Tunnel is also composed of PACT-track. Long, westbound trains sometimes have one or two robot locomotives midtrain. If required to stop at the signal just east of the Mount Macdonald Tunnel, train engineers must ensure that the midtrain robot units are clear of the Mount Shaughnessy Tunnel. The Shaughnessy Tunnel has no supplemental ventilation. A couple of robot locomotives idling in the tunnel soon deplete the fresh air, causing the units to overheat and shut down.

As Below, So Above

When confronted with the grade reduction problems of the Rogers Pass Project, CP Rail developed innovative solutions on its open track. Crews excavated almost two million cubic yards of material along 8.5 miles of sidehills for the Macdonald Track in the Beaver River valley. In places, retaining walls more than thirty feet high were required to stabilize the cuts—220,000 square feet of walls were built. On a one-mile-long section of the new track, the side slope approached forty degrees. From both engineering and environmental

☆ When it Rains ... ☆

The steep, constricted terrain of the Selkirk Mountains also threatens CP Rail's Rogers Pass operations in the summer. Not a year goes by without a mudslide or debris flow washing out a section of the rails. As at many other locations in BC, the years 1894 and 1936 recorded extensive flooding and many washouts, but the events of July 1983 are legendary for the railway line in Rogers Pass. On the heels of the profound El Niño that began in 1982, and one of the colder springtimes in BC history, 140 millimetres of rain fell in the Rogers Pass area between July 12 and July 15, 1983. In one twenty-four-hour period during the storm, 93.5 millimetres of rain fell at the Mount Fidelity weather station (elevation 1,875 metres),

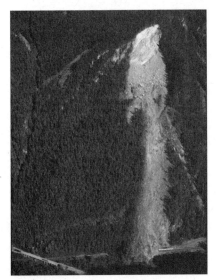

and 82 millimetres of rain fell at Rogers Pass park headquarters (elevation 1,325 metres). These were all-time, single-day records for both stations. Environment Canada subsequently estimated that such rainfalls were likely to occur once every 220 years.

At higher elevations, much of the rain fell on snow that had yet to melt, increasing the magnitude of the runoff. The deluge washed away gauging stations, and washed out or damaged at least six highway and railway bridges near Rogers Pass. Along the thirty miles between Revelstoke and the west portal of the Connaught Tunnel, CP Rail's line was breached in thirteen places. Debris flows covered the track at twenty-five other locations. The line was closed from July 12 to July 19. Just twenty-three hours after the line reopened, a 100-foot section of track collapsed into the Illecillewaet River when another eighty millimetres of rain fell. Closures of the line and adjacent the Trans-Canada Highway continued until July 24. More than one hundred people worked around the clock on the railway reconstruction, which used more than two thousand cars of ballast and rock fill.

---

viewpoints, this was far too steep for cut-and-fill construction. Undercutting the slope would have threatened the Connaught Track above, and the Trans-Canada Highway below, as well as creating the risk of landslides into the Beaver River. As this section of the line was within Glacier National Park, CP Rail had to answer to environmental guidelines—Parks Canada had stipulated that the "footprint" of the project could be no more than 97.5 feet wide. The engineering vice-president in charge of the project, John Fox, proposed a solution that was later named for him—the John Fox Viaduct.

The viaduct begins one-half of a mile railway-west of Stoney Creek bridge, and runs for 4,032 feet to a point that is 1,056 feet from the east portal of the Mount Shaughnessy Tunnel. The viaduct consists of forty-five steel spans that rest on forty-four concrete piers and two massive concrete abutments. The piers range in height from fifteen to seventy feet. Work on the piers began in 1985 and was completed the following year. Crews completed installation of the steel spans, each of which is 89.2 feet long and weighs 80.7 tons, on July 16, 1987. The spans were too long to be shipped through the Spiral Tunnels on the main line, so special trains carried them from Calgary through Crowsnest Pass and the Columbia Valley to Golden. The John Fox Viaduct and the Rogers Pass Project carried their first revenue traffic—a westbound coal train—at noon on December 12, 1988.

11
No Help Wanted

The story of helper locomotive operations at Rogers Pass exemplifies that nothing is constant in railroading. During the days of steam, helper locomotives operated from Beavermouth on the eastern approach to the pass, and from Albert Canyon on the western approach. Those based at Beavermouth assisted trains at least as far as Stoney Creek, but often ran across the pass to Glacier station, where they were cut out. On the western approach, helpers usually ran to Glacier or to the Rogers Pass station. On some heavy trains, helpers were added at Donald or at Revelstoke to assist with the entire crossing of the pass. With the abandonment of above-ground operations in Rogers Pass following the completion of the Connaught Tunnel in 1916, the new Glacier station, just west of the tunnel, became the cut-out point for both eastbound and westbound helpers, because the new crest of the climb was just inside the west portal of the tunnel.

In 1974, completion of the Mica Dam on the Columbia River created Kinbasket Reservoir. CP Rail relocated 8.3 miles of track to above the high waterline, abandoned Beavermouth, and moved the helper locomotive base a short distance west to Rogers siding. For the last fourteen years of their operations on the eastern approach to Rogers Pass, helpers plied the 9.8 miles of track between Rogers and Stoney Creek, which had an average grade of 1.98 percent, and a ruling grade of 2.2 percent.

☆ Roadies, Robots, Helpers, and Slaves ☆

Train crews and train fans have nicknames for locomotives, depending on where the engines are coupled in a train. Road locomotives are those at the head end. The unit out front "rides point." In the steam era, an engineer, brakeman, fireman, and conductor usually worked as a team, assigned to a particular locomotive. As the number of locomotives and the frequency of traffic increased, this tradition ended, but the engineer assigned to a train would often arrange the road locomotives. For instance, he might have put a cleaner burning unit on the point. Contemporary engineers also arrange the lash-ups, but for different reasons—for instance, some locomotives have better sightlines to the rear, making it easier for the crew to monitor the train. There are no extra eyes at the rear on modern trains. CP Rail removed cabooses from regular service in 1990.

With the advent of diesel-electric locomotives, longer and heavier trains became possible, but due to the extreme forces on the draw-bars between freight cars far back in the train, CP Rail found that no more than four locomotives could be placed at the head end. These locomotives often did not have sufficient pulling power for the mountain grades and desired payloads, so, in 1967, the company began experimenting with remote-controlled locomotives (initially called robots, then called slaves, now called DPUs—distributed power units) placed about two-thirds of the way back in the train. These un-crewed units were initially hardwired but are now radio-controlled from the point, by a system called Locotrol.

A peculiar feature of mountain railroading is that on long freight trains the road locomotives may be braking at the beginning of a downhill grade while the slave units are still under power, yet to crest the preceding climb. When this occurs, the Locotrol system is set to "independent mode." Otherwise, it is set to "multiple-unit mode." In the early days, draw-bars often broke toward the rear of the train due to the forces created when the transition point between acceleration and deceleration moved back and forth along the train. CP Rail found that if it coupled the slave units (there were often three or four) about midway in the train, all the cars were held in tension, and broken draw-bars became rare. Until the mid-1990s, most of the slaves operated by CP Rail were in the SD40-2 or GP-38 classes and were easily recognized because their windows were covered. Today, with more sophisticated power-handling technology available, CP Rail often couples a pair of DPUs at the rear of a train for the run between Calgary to Revelstoke.

Locomotives added to a train to assist with climbing or descending a specific grade are known as helpers in Canada, as pushers in the US, and as bankers in the UK. Canadian Pacific no longer operates any dedicated helper locomotives. They are only added to trains on special assignments or to assist when other locomotives break down.

A typical westbound, 112-car coal train, weighing 14,500 tons—or a 106-car grain train, weighing 12,000 tons—was each powered by six locomotives as it pulled into Rogers siding. The train would have had four road locomotives out front and two slave units behind the forty-sixth car. Six SD40-2 helper locomotives were added behind the eighty-first car. (On express freights of 4,200 tons or less, the helpers would be coupled ahead of the road locomotives; an arrangement crews called a "nose job.")

Although each locomotive generated three thousand horsepower and was run wide open on the climb, the top speed possible with thirty-six thousand horsepower engaged was about twenty-five miles per hour. This would ebb to fifteen miles per hour as a train approached Stoney Creek. After being cut out of the train, the helper crew would wait on siding track for instructions to return to Rogers siding during a lull in traffic. Back at Rogers, they would get some sleep, have a meal, or pick up their next assignment.

Completion of the Rogers Pass Project in 1988 reduced the westbound climb to 0.98 percent—at the time, well within the capabilities of five or six locomotives assigned to heavy freight trains. This spelled the end for the Rogers helper locomotive base—the last on CP Rail's main line. Its siding track became part of the new double-track. Because of the greater power of contemporary locomotives, eastbound trains, which are generally empty, now also run over Rogers Pass without assistance. They typically use the Connaught Track, which has a maximum uphill grade of 2.4 percent west of the pass, and a maximum downhill grade of 2.2 percent east of the pass. The occasional eastbound train that is loaded (usually with lumber) will be powered from Revelstoke to Calgary by a lash-up of as many as six locomotives at the head end. These trains are limited to about sixty cars to preclude the

CP locomotive 5939 was coupled ahead of 5938 in this typical lash-up of SD40-2 helpers, photographed in 1994 at the west end of the Field yard. Both locomotives were manufactured by EMD in 1979. Locomotive 5938 had the fresher paint job in this view, but it was subsequently wrecked, while, as of 2009, locomotive 5939 carried on in service.

necessity of adding helpers. Dispatchers sometimes run trains on the "wrong track" across Rogers Pass—westbound on the Connaught Track; eastbound on the Macdonald Track. The scheduling of time-sensitive freight is one of the governing factors in track assignment, however, dispatchers and crews must ensure that a train's locomotives can generate sufficient braking power for the downhill grades.

The double-tracking of the Rogers Pass Project not only increased capacity by 60 percent (by increasing the frequency of trains), it also improved the speed of freight shipments. The "push" up the grade from Rogers alone required thirty-five to forty minutes. Engaging and disengaging helper locomotives added an additional two hours to the passage of each assisted train. CP Rail's accounting staff probably appreciated some of the other improvements that came with the demise of the helper service. Gone were the maintenance and fuel costs for the fleet of eighteen SD40-2 helpers, each of which had required $1 million per year to operate. The locomotives each guzzled 167 gallons of diesel per hour while working; their 3,340-gallon tanks had required filling four times a week. Also gone was the highest paid locomotive posting with CP Rail: the helper engineer at Rogers siding. This was something of a double saving, as both members of a helper crew were engineers who took alternate shifts as brakemen.

☆ The Workhorses ☆

Today, Canadian Pacific operates more than 1,600 diesel-electric locomotives. General Motors Electro-Motive Division (EMD) of London, Ontario, built many of the locomotives that run across Rogers Pass. Until the mid-1990s, the most numerous locomotive type on CP and on railways throughout North America was the SD40-2 class (3,957 have been built), introduced in 1972. An SD40-2 ("SD" means "special duty") generates three thousand horsepower, has three-axle trucks, and three roof-mounted cooling fans. It has 40-inch diameter wheels; an overall length of 68 feet, 10 inches; and weighs 368,000 pounds. CP Rail took possession of 484 of these locomotives as new purchases, and acquired more through absorption of the Delaware and Hudson Railway in 1991, and the Soo Line in 1992. The bulk of CP Rail's SD40-2 locomotives bear numbers between 5490 and 6623.

The other locomotive stalwart was the GP38-2 class. CP Rail purchased 136 new GP38-2 locomotives from EMD in the early 1970s, and acquired more through the above-noted mergers ("GP" means "general purpose"). Still in use, each generates two thousand horsepower. You may see these units from time to time on the Rogers Pass grades. Most of them are numbered between 3000 and 4526.

In 1989, CP Rail purchased twenty-five SD40-2F locomotives from EMD, num-

Still factory-fresh, Canadian Pacific's locomotive 9616— an AC4400 CW manufactured by General Electric—rolls west from Field on its way toward Rogers Pass, in November 1997.

bered from 9000 to 9024. The wide design of the cab increased crew comfort significantly, allowing the engineer, brakeman, and conductor to ride together at a time when cabooses were being removed from regular service. When it was new to CP Rail, crews often desired that an SD40-SF be "on the point" as the lead road locomotive. The increase in comfort came at a cost. Because of its greater width, the SD40-2F offered only limited visibility to the rear. As with some of the SD40-2s, the SD40-2Fs have diagonal red and white striping on their front cowlings. Because of its wider profile, train buffs know the SD40-2F as a "red barn."

The move to greater horsepower continued in the late 1990s. CP operates sixty-one SD90MAC/43 locomotives, built by EMD in 1998, and numbered from 9100 to 9160. These generate 4,300 horsepower. Units 9112-9160 were acquired as kits that CP assembled at its Ogden Shops in Calgary. Each could be upgraded to six thousand horsepower, but the railway has not done so. CP reduced its original order for SD90MAC-H locomotives in 1999, taking only four units instead of twenty. These were numbered from 9300 to 9303. Each generated six thousand horsepower. They were removed from service in the summer of 2008. General Motors sold its EMD in April 2005. The new company is called "Electro-Motive Diesel," so the EMD designation has not disappeared from new locomotives it manufactures.

Since the 1960s, General Electric (GE) has been the principal competitor to EMD in the North American locomotive market. CP operates 438 of GE's AC4400CW locomotives. These are numbered 9500 to 9683 (acquired between 1995 and 1998); 8500 to 8580 (acquired in 1998); 8600 to 8655 (acquired in 2001); 9700 to 9740 (acquired in 2002); 9750 to 9784 (acquired in 2003); and 9800 to 9840 (acquired in 2004). As its name implies, this type of locomotive generates 4,400 horsepower. GE built 2,598 of these units. They are in service on all but two of North America's major railroads.

Headed by locomotive 8850, an ES44AC GEVO, a westbound stack train exits the Mount Macdonald Tunnel. The Connaught track is on the right.

General Electric's most recent entry into the high-horsepower locomotive market is the ES44AC, which replaces the AC4400CW. Canadian Pacific began taking delivery of an order of 200 units in 2005, with delivery completed in 2008. The newer of the ES44AC locomotives are "Evolution" series units—known to train buffs as GEVOs—which meet the US standards for diesel emissions. They have 12-cylinder engines compared to the 16-cylinder engines of the older models, yet produce the same horsepower while using less fuel and creating 40 percent fewer emissions. GE claims that if every freight train in North America were harnessed to a GEVO, the annual reduction in nitrogen oxide emissions would be equivalent to removing 48 million passenger cars from highways. Canadian Pacific's ES44AC units bear the numbers from 8700 to 8899. The railway ordered 110 more of these locomotives for delivery by 2010.

With the greater horsepower available, the typical lash-up of locomotives on trains in the Rockies and Selkirks has changed. It is not uncommon to see two SD90MAC, AC4400 CW, or ES44AC locomotives on the head end of a loaded train, and two in service as robots at the rear, with none mid-train. These units accomplish the work formerly tackled by seven SD40-2 units. But the SD40-2 locomotive remains the "slant six" of Canadian Pacific's locomotive fleet. Although they generate less power and are less fuel efficient, they are more reliable than the newer, more complex locomotives. As stories elsewhere in this book testify, reliability rules in railroading.

12

The Hill

Every major railroad has at least one incline that is the dread of design engineers, construction engineers, and locomotive engineers. The CPR initially had two. The Big Hill, which descended 1,140 feet in 7.55 miles from the crest of the Continental Divide to Field, had a ruling grade of 4.5 percent. It was an outright railroading horror, where steam and metal went head-on with gravity. By contrast, the grade west of Rogers Pass, known simply as "the Hill," descended 3,081 feet in about forty-five miles, with ruling grades of 2.4 percent and an average grade of 1.3 percent. Its tangle with gravity, though much less spectacular, was protracted. From the simple point of view of physics, more could go wrong in a run of two hours than in a run of one hour, and it frequently did. Add the fact that avalanche slopes threatened much of the Hill, and the prospects for calamity increased.

The CPR never took train operations on the Hill lightly, and neither does Canadian Pacific (CP) today. The packet of orders for locomotive engineers is complex; governing speed and braking on different trains under different conditions, and on different sections of the grade. For most of the descent to Revelstoke, the maximum speed permitted is twenty miles per hour. On a 110-car train weighing more than fifteen thousand tons, an engineer can only maintain this maximum through judicious applications of air brakes and dynamic engine-braking, alternating with brief applications of power.

Accounts of disasters and near disasters on the Hill are legion, but one stands apart as a chronicle of destruction and providence. To Revelstoke rail-

Selkirk-type, Class T1a, locomotive 5904 derailed on The Hill in 1936 but was returned to service.

In its battle with The Hill, the CPR has never taken rest from improving the efficiency and safety of the track. Here, a bridge crew rebuilt one of the crossings of the Illecillewaet River in 1900. Timbers again gave way to steel.

roaders it became known as "Timmy Hamm's wreck." Hamm was the engineer on CP Rail Extra 5820 West, just after midnight on November 26, 1977, as it waited at Glacier siding for clear track to begin the run to Revelstoke. A lash-up of four SD40-2 road locomotives powered the head end, with four robot units midtrain. The payload of 106 full coal cars and the caboose at the tail gave a total weight to the train of 15,292 tons. Hamm's crew in the cab included brakeman Greg Tirrell and engineer trainee Clarence Thacker. Rear brakeman Jimmy Gullickson and conductor Bill Belton crewed the caboose, more than a mile to the rear.

Snow was piling up on the tracks—more than a foot had fallen during the evening. When the signal at the west end of the siding changed to give Extra 5820 clear track, Thacker released the air brakes. The train began to roll forward on the 1.5 percent grade. CP Rail's regulations required a brake application soon after leaving Glacier to hold the train to ten miles per hour. Thacker waited until the train reached fifteen miles per hour before making the first attempt at braking. Although everyone in the cab heard the discharge of the air brakes, the train continued to pick up speed. Engineer Hamm told Thacker to brake again. He did, but the train had accelerated to thirty-five miles per hour by the time it was 1.5 miles below Glacier.

Under normal circumstances, Thacker had applied the brakes enough to bring the train to a stop. Everyone on the train knew something was wrong, but Gullickson, calling the cab from the caboose, was the first to voice the thought: "Have you got hold of her?" Thacker replied, "We're working on it." Timmy Hamm knew they were riding a runaway. He ordered Thacker to apply the emergency brake. It, too, was ineffective.

When Hamm informed Belton and Gullickson that the emergency brake had failed, the two men donned their parkas and prepared to jump into the night. Standing on the front pier of the caboose, Belton realized he had forgotten to put on his boots. He went back inside for them, leaving Gullickson to contemplate the leap into the murky blur of blowing snow, trees, and rocks as the train picked up speed to sixty miles per hour. By the time Belton rejoined him, the pair knew that to jump would be suicide. In the locomotive cab, despite Hamm's caution not to jump, Thacker and Tirrell were also grabbing their coats. They opened the rear door of the cab, but the blast of icy air and snow, and the prospect of landing their jumps into a cliff or into the Illecillewaet River sent them back inside.

Looking ahead, the locomotive crew saw the signal at Flat Creek siding. They no longer had clear track. An eastbound freight was just ahead and they should have been pulling into the siding to stop and let it go by. Their runaway had just morphed into a candidate for a high-speed, head-on collision. As the train reached the impossible speed of seventy miles per hour, the locomotives automatically shut down. At the rear of the train, Gullickson crawled forward to successfully disconnect the caboose. Conductor and rear brakeman were now riding their own one-car runaway, with the application of two manual brakes offering their only prospect for survival. If that failed, the men fully expected they would soon be ploughing into the rear of the wreckage of Extra 5820.

In the control room in Revelstoke, the dispatcher had been anxiously watching Extra 5820's rapid progress down the Hill. She radioed the engineer of the eastbound freight, advising him that 5820 was a runaway and that he should get his train into Illecillewaet siding, 13.2 miles west of Glacier, as soon as he could. The eastbound engineer gave his train maximum power, speeding uphill toward the runaway in order to get out of its way.

Whether he would have made it will never be known. As Extra 5820 crested eighty-five miles per hour on a curve east of Illecillewaet siding, the drawbar behind the third locomotive snapped. The fourth locomotive lurched sideways, left the track, and flipped over into the river, followed by seventy-eight coal cars and the four robot locomotives. As the lead locomotives began to slow, Hamm, Thacker, and Tirrell realized they had survived the derailment—at least temporarily. They expected at least one coal car would make it through the chaos of twisted steel and exploding locomotives behind them to smash into the rear of their lash-up. None came. Belton and Gullickson also escaped death, saved by their efforts at the manual brake wheels, which brought them to a halt, averting a collision with the derailment.

In less than eight minutes, Extra 5820 had run more than eight miles of track and negotiated twenty-four curves on grades that reached 2.4 percent. The derailment destroyed two bridges, the rail bed, and the trackside telephone lines. In the days before "environmental disaster" was part of the dialect, the wreck epitomized the term as thousands of gallons of flaming diesel poured into the Illecillewaet River and clouds of acrid smoke choked the valley. The clean-up required ten days. The total cost of the destruction was more than $6 million—at the time, the most expensive train wreck in Canadian history. In its report on the derailment, released in 1980, the Canadian Transportation Safety Board cited the three senior members of the crew as being responsible for the runaway. Their union disputed the findings. Eventually, CP Rail instituted new procedures for air brake training and application.

The crew of Extra 5820 seemed to have had horseshoes with them in November 1977, but not all who work the Hill near Illecillewaet have been so lucky. In the spring of 1935, two days of heavy rain saturated the snow in the Illecillewaet Valley, releasing massive avalanches that stripped many trees from the slopes. The following winter, avalanche activity in the valley increased. In the middle of the night on February 28, 1936, T1a, Selkirk-type locomotive 5911, derailed in a slide between Illecillewaet and Downie sidings. The snow deposit was three hundred feet long and fifteen feet deep. After working for forty-eight hours, a shovelling gang uncovered the tender, which they cut from the engine. To make more room for the crew, an auxiliary locomotive towed the tender east (uphill) on the track, using a cable and hook.

A mile above the derailment site, the tender broke loose and ran back into the cut where men were still shovelling. The impact killed fifteen in the cut and one man who jumped from the tender into the Illecillewaet River, accounting for the second-highest death toll in one incident on the CPR. Five others were taken to the hospital in Revelstoke. Most of the labourers who survived had cheated death by taking an unauthorized smoke break behind a boulder just upslope from the cut. A coroner's jury returned a verdict of accidental death but recommended that the CPR install a derailing device uphill from crews working in any similar circumstances.

☆ Off the Rails ☆

On the grades on either side of Rogers Pass, nature often deals the blow that derails a train—whether it be an avalanche, rockfall, or debris flow. However, as locomotives become more powerful and trains become longer and heavier, physics and human error emerge frequently as the causes of derailments.

If you have heard a train pulling away from a station or shuttling about in a siding, you may recall the sound that falls like audible dominoes along a train's length as it begins to move. This sound comes from the "play" in the drawbars that couple locomotives and cars to each other. As a train gets underway, the power of the lead locomotive(s) pulls the first car ahead. Then the weight and momentum of the powered unit(s) and that car begin to propel the second car, and so on. As each car begins to accelerate, the drawbar behind it takes up "slack," both where it is connected to the car through a spring-loaded gear, and at the knuckle, the point where the drawbar is connected to the drawbar of the next car. This makes the noise you hear, although skilled engineers pride themselves in getting a train underway quietly. Drawbar slack is essential to a train's ability to move. If all the drawbars in a long, stationary train on level grade were stretched tight (a condition railroaders call draft force), no amount of locomotive power would set the train in motion. There are times when this happens and an engineer has to "jiggle" a train to unscramble the drawbars and "get some slack."

As a train moves through the mountains, different parts can be on different aspects of grade—the road locomotives can be beginning to descend a grade (taking up slack) while the rest of the train is holding the slack on level grade or just cresting a climb. The engineer must control the throttling and engine-braking of the road locomotives and any robot locomotives accordingly. If the engineer misjudges the power requirements, two things might happen. Drawbar knuckles can be broken apart, segmenting the train. This should result in an automatic application of air brakes to the separated part of the train—not something an engineer wants on a résumé but preferable to the disaster that results from "straight-lining." When the engineer applies too much power and the drawbars on a section of train all tighten, the cars may take the straightest line between two points on a shallow curve and actually lift from the rails. This inevitably derails those cars and causes the following cars to pile into the derailment. Although many factors can contribute to straight-lining, the engineer usually takes the rap for some lapse in power management that permits the metal and mass of physics to run their grinding course.

☆ Uphill, Downhill ☆

Westbound trains in the days of steam were not finished with steep grades when they reached Revelstoke. To the west, the track climbed 285 feet in 8.2 miles to Clanwilliam siding at the crest of Eagle Pass. The average grade was 0.65 percent, but the ruling grade was close to 2 percent for the 4.1 miles between the Begbie and Tum Tum sidings. Helper locomotives were required. The single track created delays, with the helpers having to await a clear track for the run back to Revelstoke. To minimize such inefficiency, the CPR attempted to avoid running helper locomotives "light."

The following chronicles a typical day in the life of Selkirk helper 5923 (see photo on page 116) in the twilight of the steam era, in the late 1940s. Departing Revelstoke in the morning, 5923 assisted the eastbound passenger train, the Dominion, 108.7 miles to Leanchoil siding (16.9 miles west of Field)—a trip that took four and a half hours to complete. The crew turned 5923 on the wye at Leanchoil where the unit waited about forty minutes to pick up a helper assignment with the westbound Dominion. The trip back to Revelstoke took just

A shovelling gang pauses partway through the job of excavating a lash-up of two locomotives on The Hill near Rogers Pass in 1886. The lead locomotive, 365, was a Consolidation-type 4-4-0 that had entered service in July that year. It survived the mishap and eventually logged forty years and three months of service.

over four hours. If 5923 was not needed to help the Dominion farther west, it would be cut out at Revelstoke, but often it remained with the train for the climb to Clanwilliam, or to Taft, 23.4 miles west, so as to be available to assist a heavy eastbound train down the grade to Revelstoke. When the crew walked away from 5923 after such a day, they had been out for more than twelve hours and had covered almost 266 miles.

In 1979, CP Rail double-tracked the 4.1 miles immediately west of Revelstoke, reducing the ruling grade on the westbound track to 1.1 percent, decreasing the need for helpers and eliminating the single-track bottleneck.

The archetype of Canadian Pacific's locomotive steam power in its archetypical setting: Selkirk-type, Class T1b, 5923, waits on siding track at the west portal of Connaught Tunnel in the late 1930s. Mount Sir Donald is in the background.

13
On Track—
A Railway History
Walking Guide

For its key role in Canadian transportation, Rogers Pass was designated a National Historic Site in 1974. Stretching from Stoney Creek to Loop Brook, and from the valley bottoms to the mountain tops, by area, it is one of the larger National Historic Sites in Canada. With all railway operations at the crest of Rogers Pass now underground, there are no opportunities for conventional trainspotting. However, several sections of the original railway grade have been converted into walking trails, allowing you to put "boots to rail bed" to explore history. Remember to take the necessary precautions for travel in bear country. Please note that decreased maintenance and funding in Glacier National Park means that signs for some of these trailheads and viewpoints may be missing. Highway and trail distances are given below in kilometres (km).

☆ At the **Stone Arch Bridge Viewpoint,** 7.3 km east of Rogers Pass, you can see the bridge built in 1898 across Cascade Creek (see photo on page 63). The east portal of the Connaught Tunnel is nearby, below the highway grade.

☆ At the **Tractor Shed Picnic Area**, 2.6 km east of Rogers Pass, you can view the ruins of 10 Shed. The spectacularly confined terrain of the east

The ruins of 10 Shed at the Tractor Shed Picnic Area in August 2006.

entrance to the pass towers above. Mount Macdonald is to the south; Mount Tupper is to the north.

☆ **The Abandoned Rails Trail** begins on the east side of the Rogers Pass Discovery Centre and runs south for 1.6 km to the Trans-Canada Highway exhibit at the crest of Rogers Pass. You can examine the ruins of 16 Shed and 17 Shed. Railway ties, which were not removed when the trail was laid on top of them, are thinly concealed by the tread surface. The trail is wheelchair accessible with assistance.

☆ **The 1885 Trail** (3.8 km) connects the Illecillewaet and Loop Brook campgrounds, and provides quick access to Glacier House National Historic Site. Turn into Illecillewaet campground, 3.7 km west of the Rogers Pass Discovery centre. Drive straight ahead on the access road (built on top of the original railway grade) to the parking lot and kiosk at the rear of the campground. Walk uphill a short distance on a gated gravel road and turn right. Exhibits in the first two hundred metres describe the history and construction of the Canadian Pacific Railway. The trail crosses the Illecillewaet River on a stone arch bridge, completed in 1900.

The highlight of the trail is Glacier House National Historic Site, where more displays describe the construction and the operation of the CPR hotel. Many artifacts remain. Beyond the site of Glacier House,

This Vaux Family photograph shows the "Glacier Creek" bridge (first crossing of the Illecillewaet River) under construction on July 14, 1900. Note the trestle in the background, which the bridge would replace.

The "Glacier Creek" bridge (first crossing of the Illecillewaet River) in August 2006, 106 years after its construction.

follow the trail downhill on the 2.2 percent grade to Loop Brook campground, passing several clay culverts and the remains of eight snowsheds (numbers 21 to 28). About one kilometre west of the site of Glacier House, the west portal of the Connaught Tunnel is concealed from view on the valley floor. You may hear trains as they enter and exit the tunnel. You will certainly hear the highway traffic. At the junction on the east edge of Loop Brook campground, you may descend steeply to your right to the trail's end at the parking area on the Trans-Canada Highway, passing some of the stone columns of The Loops, or continue straight ahead to make a circuit of the campground on The Loops grade. This will add 1.6 km to the outing. Retrace your route (uphill) to Illecillewaet campground, or pre-arrange transportation for the end of your walk.

☆ **The Loop Brook Trail** is 6.5 km west of the Rogers Pass Discovery Centre. The trail makes a 1.6-km circuit of Loop Brook campground, following the original grade of the middle third of the Loops. It allows for close-up viewing of the stone columns that were completed in 1906 to replace the timber and fill trestles. The trail also takes you past the ruins of 27 Shed and 28 Shed. This part of The Loops crossed Loop Brook twice. Five columns supported the southern trestle; eight columns supported the northern trestle. After The Loops were abandoned, ·Loop Brook undermined one of the southerly columns. The column lies virtually intact where it toppled, testifying to the stonework. You can look for stone masons' marks on the massive blocks of the columns. To the north across the valley, there are two sets of columns that supported the westernmost third of The Loops on its crossings of the Illecillewaet River. Keen-eyed spotters may pick out these columns in spring and autumn when the leaves are off the trees.

You can visit Parks Canada's Rogers Pass Discovery Centre at Rogers Pass, the Revelstoke Railway Museum (http://www.railwaymuseum.com), and the Revelstoke Museum and Archives (http://www.revelstokemuseum. ca) in Revelstoke for more information on the railway history of Rogers Pass. At Craigellachie National Historic Site, forty-five kilometres west of Revelstoke on the Trans-Canada Highway, you can visit the site where Donald Smith drove the "last spike" in the construction of the CPR on November 7, 1885.

If you would like to check the weather at Rogers Pass, visit: http://www.th.gov.bc.ca/bchighwaycam/index.aspx?cam=101

For the Revelstoke weather forecast online, visit: http://www.weatheroffice.gc.ca/city/pages/bc-65_metric_e.html

"The Wing," Glacier House and its disappearing glacier in 1909.

The footings for "The Wing" in August 2006.

Selected Place Names near Rogers Pass

Afton. The name of this mountain, which rises above the site of Glacier House, is an amalgam of the surnames of Phillip Abbot, Charles Fay, and Charles Thompson, members of the Appalachian Mountain Club who frequented Glacier House in the 1890s.

Albert Canyon. Albert Rogers was the nephew of, and in 1881 was the assistant to, surveyor Albert Bowman Rogers.

Beavermouth. Although it would make sense that this early CPR construction community and later railway siding were sited at the mouth of the Beaver River at its confluence with the Columbia River, Beavermouth was actually just upstream from there, at the mouth of Quartz Creek.

Begbie. This 2,732-metre-high peak was named for "the hanging judge," Sir Matthew Baillie Begbie, chief justice of British Columbia from 1870 to1899.

Big Eddy. This locality on the west bank of the Columbia River opposite Revelstoke was named after a feature on the river.

Carroll. The original name for the mountain now called Mount Macdonald was bestowed in honour of a member of Major Rogers's surveying party.

Cheops. This 2,583-metre-high mountain was named for a fancied resemblance to the Great Pyramid at Giza, the burial place of the Egyptian pharaoh Cheops.

Clanwilliam. Richard James Meade was a British mariner who married a daughter of the governor of Vancouver Island in 1870, and who became the Earl of Clanwilliam in 1879. The Clanwilliam siding is the high point in Eagle Pass.

Columbia. Captain Robert Gray, the first American to circumnavigate the world, named this river for his vessel, *Columbia Rediviva*, which anchored at the river's mouth and laid US claim in May 1792.

Craigellachie. Located on the River Spey in Scotland, the original Craigellachie (kreg-AH-leh-key) was the ancestral home of George Stephen, the first president of the CPR. Craigellachie, in Eagle Pass, BC, was where the "last spike" of the CPR was driven, on November 7, 1885.

Donald. This settlement at "First Crossing" was named for Donald Alexander Smith, Lord Strathcona, a director of the CPR during its construction.

Downie. The siding was named for Thomas Downie, a superintendent on the CPR, who was killed nearby in an avalanche, prior to 1939.

Eagle. Surveyor Walter Moberly saw eagles fly over a river that emptied into Shuswap Lake. The river and the pass that it led to were later named accordingly.

Illecillewaet. *Illecillewaet* is a Syilx (Okanagan) First Nations word meaning "swift water."

Macdonald. This 2,893-metre-high mountain and the 9.11-mile-long tunnel were named for John Alexander Macdonald, who served as the first and third prime minister of Canada, and who spirited the construction of the CPR.

Revelstoke. The closest settlement to Rogers Pass was named for Edward Charles Baring, the First Baron Revelstoke. He was a principal in the British bank that issued a series of bonds in the spring of 1885, the proceeds from which financed the completion of the CPR.

Rogers. The siding, the 3,189-metre-high peak, and the 1,330-metre-high pass were named for Albert Bowman Rogers, CPR surveyor.

Ross. This 2,301-metre-high peak that rises above The Loops was named for James Ross, construction superintendent of the CPR in western Canada, and the man responsible for laying track across Rogers Pass.

Sifton. This 2,940-metre-high mountain was named in 1901 for Clifford Sifton, Canada's Minister of the Interior, 1896-1905.

Sir Donald. Originally known as Syndicate Peak, this 3,297-metre-high mountain that towers over Rogers Pass was named for Donald Alexander Smith (see also entry for Donald), Lord Strathcona, who was knighted for his role as a CPR director during the railway's construction.

Taft. According to the BC Geographical Names Office, this siding was named for William Howard Taft, the twenty-seventh president of the US who was elected in 1908, just prior to the construction of the siding. Local lore has it that the siding was named for a Mr. Taft of the Hood Lumber Company.

Tangier. This river and the pass at its head take their names from a mining claim staked in 1895.

Three Valley. The three valleys that intersect at this location west of Rogers Pass are those of Tonkawatla Creek, Eagle River, and South Pass Creek.

Tum Tum. This siding name is a local, unofficial name for Tonkawatla Creek. Many First Nations use the expression *Tum Tum* to describe a watercourse with waterfalls.

Tupper. This 2,816-metre-high summit on the north side of the eastern entrance to Rogers Pass was named for Charles Tupper, Minister of Railways and Canals in John A. Macdonald's governments, and later Canada's seventh prime minister.

Sources

A writer who takes on any aspect of the genesis and construction of the Canadian Pacific Railway (CPR) owes a monumental debt to the late Pierre Berton's one-two punch, *The National Dream* and *The Last Spike*. I used Berton's research to help frame the political backdrop to the CPR, and for information on the Pacific Survey. Walter Moberly's *The Rocks and Rivers of British Columbia*, written in 1885, and his *History of the C.P.R. Road*, written ca. 1909, provided the background on his endeavours. Tom Wilson's *Trailblazer of the Canadian Rockies*, and A. O. Wheeler's *The Selkirk Range, Volume 1* provided information on Major Albert Bowman Rogers and the surveying fieldwork for the CPR. The appendices of Wheeler's work contain Albert Rogers's account of the 1881 expedition, many observations made by early visitors to the area of Rogers Pass, weather records from Glacier House, and an extract from James White's *Altitudes of Canada*, which presents a valuable mileage and elevation chart for the CPR before construction of the Connaught Tunnel.

Much of the anecdotal information on railway operations and events in Rogers Pass came from various files at the Revelstoke Railway Museum, and at the Revelstoke Museum Archives. Each of these archives holds extensive material on the Connaught Tunnel, the Rogers Pass Project, and on the March 1910 avalanche. The Revelstoke Museum Archives contains a definitive discussion of the death toll of that latter event. The account of the 1929

Surprise Creek bridge collapse is based on material available at the Revelstoke Museum Archives; that of "Timmy Hamm's wreck" is based on material found at the Revelstoke Railway Museum.

I relied upon Robert Turner's *West of the Great Divide*, and the late Omer Lavallée's *Van Horne's Road* for specific information concerning railway operations in Rogers Pass. I found these volumes invaluable for their meticulous chronologies of construction and related events, particularly snowshed construction and the building of the bridges in the Beaver River valley, and the firestorm of 1886. The research of these authors also helped me to keep a handle on the frequent changes to the above-ground routing of the rails in the pass, and the various incarnations of the Rogers Pass station and yards. *Van Horne's Road* contains many quotations from James Ross's letters to William Cornelius Van Horne. I used its photo credits as a cross-reference to properly attribute the historical photos in this work.

Titles published by the British Railway Modellers of North America—the ten volumes of Donald Bain's *Canadian Pacific in the Rockies*, the two volumes of *Canadian Pacific in the Selkirks* by Jan Booth and Roger Steed, and Donald Bain and Jack Leslie's *Canadian Pacific's Mighty No. 8000*—provided wonderful details on railway operations in the pass, and particulars about locomotives, equipment, and events.

David Mattison has compiled colossal research on photographers who worked along the CPR in the late nineteenth and early twentieth centuries in *Camera Workers: The British Columbia, Alaska & Yukon Photographic Directory, 1858-1950—Volume 1*, which can be found on the Internet at http://members.shaw.ca/bchistorian/cw1858-1950.html. I was often able to combine Mattison's research with details in specific images to better place those photographs in their physical and historical contexts.

I frequently consulted Ray Verdone's website, *CPR Steam Locomotives Database*, at http://CPRsteam.org, for specifics about individual locomotives, and it was there I found Jonathan Hanna's concise but detailed history of the T4a, locomotive 8000. Although it may appear to readers that my head is filled with the specifics of CP Rail's train rosters, ordering dates, and numbering histories, this is not the case. The various resources available at TrainWeb.org (http://trainweb.org) were key in this regard. David Finch's *Glacier House Revisited*, William Putnam's *The Great Glacier and Its House*, and Edward Cavell's *Legacy in Ice*, along with files at the Revelstoke Museum Archives, provided the background on Glacier House. Ben Gadd faultlessly provided information on the structural geology of the Beaver River valley.

Bibliography

Bain, Donald M. *Canadian Pacific in the Rockies.* 10 vols. Calgary: British Railway Modellers of North America, 1985.

Bain, Donald M., and Jack D. Leslie. *Canadian Pacific's Mighty No. 8000.* Calgary: British Railway Modellers of North America, ca. 2003.

Berton, Pierre. *The National Dream.* Toronto: McClelland and Stewart, 1970.

---. *The Last Spike.* Toronto: McClelland and Stewart, 1971.

Blaise, Clark. *Time Lord—Sir Sandford Fleming and the Creation of Standard Time.* New York: Pantheon Books, 2000.

Booth, Jan. *Canadian Pacific in the Selkirks—100 Years in Rogers Pass.* 2nd ed. Calgary: British Railway Modellers of North America, 1991.

Bone, P. Turner. *When the Steel Went Through.* Toronto: The MacMillan Company of Canada Ltd., 1947.

Buck, George H. *From Summit to Sea.* Calgary: Fifth House, 1997.

Cavell, Edward. *Legacy in Ice—the Vaux Family and the Canadian Alps.* Banff: The Whyte Foundation, ca. 1987.

Cruise, David, and Allison Griffiths. *Lords of the Line—The Men Who Built the CPR.* Markham, ON: Penguin Books Canada, 1989.

Dennis, A. C. "Construction Methods for Rogers Pass Tunnel." In *Transactions of the American Society of Civil Engineers,* February 7, 1917.

Egan, Brian. *The Ecology of the Mountain Hemlock Zone.* Victoria: BC Ministry of Forests Research Branch, 1997.

Finch, David. *Glacier House Revisited.* Revelstoke: Friends of Mount Revelstoke and Glacier, 1991.

Fleming, Sandford. *England and Canada, A Summer Tour Between Old and New Westminister.* Montreal: Dawson Brothers, 1884.

---. *Expeditions to the Pacific, with a brief reference to the voyages of discovery in seas contiguous to Canada, in connection with a western passage from Europe to Asia.* Ottawa: Royal Society of Canada, 1889.

Grant, Rev. George M. *Ocean to Ocean—Sandford Fleming's Expedition Through Canada in 1872.* Reprint, Edmonton: M. G. Hurtig Ltd., 1967.

Green, Lorne. *Chief Engineer—Life of a Nation Builder—Sandford Fleming.* Toronto: Dundurn Press, 1993.

Lakusta, Ernie. *The Intrepid Explorer— James Hector's Explorations in the Canadian Rockies.* Calgary: Fifth House, 2007.

Lavallée, Omer. *Van Horne's Road.* Montreal: Railfare Books, 1974. Revised, 2nd ed., Toronto: Fitzhenry and Whiteside, 2007.

Mackinnon, Andy, Jim Pojar, and Ray Coupé. *Plants of Northern British Columbia.* Edmonton: Lone Pine Publishing, 1992.

McKee, Bill, and Georgeen Klassen. *Trail of Iron.* Calgary: Glenbow-Alberta Institute, 1983.

Moberly, Walter. *Early History of the C.P.R. Road,* ca. 1909; http://canyon.alanmacek.com/index.php/Moberly_(1909)_-_Text.

---. *The Rocks and Rivers of British Columbia.* London: H. Blacklock and Co., 1885.

Morris, Jackie. *Trackside Guide to CP Rail—Railway Points of Interest, Banff to Craigellachie.* Revelstoke: Friends of Mount Revelstoke and Glacier, 1993.

Pole, Graeme. *The Spiral Tunnels and the Big Hill On the Canadian Pacific Railway.* Hazelton: Mountain Vision Publishing, 2009.

---. *Great Railways of the Canadian West.* Canmore: Altitude Publishing, 2006.

Putnam, William Lowell. *The Great Glacier and Its House.* New York: The American Alpine Club, 1982.

Putnam, William L., Glen W. Boles, and Roger W. Laurilla. *Place Names of the Canadian Alps.* Revelstoke: Footprint Publishing, 1990.

Railway Investigation Report Number R02W0600, Main Track Derailment. Ottawa: Transportation Safety Board, 2002.

Roberts, Morley. *The Western Avernus.* London: J. M. Dent and Sons Ltd., 1887.

Rollins, Jon. *Caves of the Canadian Rockies and Columbia Mountains.* Calgary: Rocky Mountain Books, 2004.

Rylatt, R. M. *Surveying the Canadian Pacific.* Salt Lake City: University of Utah Press, 1991.

Secretan, J. H. E. *Canada's Great Highway: From the First Stake to the Last Spike.* London: John Lane the Bodley Head Ltd., 1924.

Shaw, Charles Æneas. *Tales of a Pioneer Surveyor.* Don Mills, ON: Longman Canada Ltd., 1970.

Sleigh, Daphne. *Walter Moberly and the Northwest Passage by Rail.* Surrey: Hancock House, 2003.

Steed, Roger G. *Canadian Pacific in the Selkirks, Volume Two.* Calgary: British Railway Modellers of North America, 1993.

Turner, Robert D. *West of the Great Divide.* 2nd ed. Winlaw, BC: Sono Nis, 2003.

Wheeler, Arthur O. *The Selkirk Range, Volume 1.* Ottawa: Department of the Interior, 1905.

Wilson, Ralph, and Don Thomas. *The Line, Calgary, Alberta to Vancouver, British Columbia.* Calgary: Canadian Pacific Railway, 1998.

Wilson, Thomas E. *Trail Blazer of the Canadian Rockies.* Calgary: Glenbow-Alberta Institute, 1972.

Yeats, Floyd. *Canadian Pacific's Big Hill.* Calgary: British Railway Modellers of North America, 1985.

Recommended Internet Resources

CPR Timeline
http://www.CPRheritage.com/history/historytxt.htm

CPR Stream Locomotives Database
http://CPRsteam.org/

Revelstoke Railway Museum
http://www.railwaymuseum.com/

Camera Workers: The British Columbia, Alaska & Yukon Photographic Directory, 1858–1950 – Volume 1
http://members.shaw.ca/bchistorian/cw1858-1950.html

Canadian Pacific Railway Locomotive Roster and Photo Archives;
http://www.trainweb.org/galt-stn/CPRoster/main.htm

Image Credits

The following abbreviations identify the sources of the photographs and illustrations.

BCA: British Columbia Archives, Royal British Columbia Museum, Victoria
CPRA: Canadian Pacific Railway Archives, Montreal
CVA: City of Vancouver Archives
GMA: Glenbow Museum Archives, Calgary
GP: © Graeme Pole/Mountain Vision
LAC: Library and Archives Canada, Ottawa
NPA: Notman Photographic Archives, McCord Museum of Canadian History, Montreal
RMA: Revelstoke Museum and Archives
RRM: Revelstoke Railway Museum
VPL: Vancouver Public Library
WMCR: Whyte Museum of the Canadian Rockies, Banff
Individual photographers are credited, when known.

Front cover *Canadian Pacific Railway* (1985) © 2008 Tucker Smith, Courtesy of the Greenwich Workshop, Inc.

Back cover and chapter "watermark image" based on O.B. Buell, CPRA A.4227

i RRM A1992-03/1
iii LAC PA-032019
2 (top) Vaux family, WMCR V653 NG-420
2 (bottom) Howard Palmer, GMA NA 3675-2
4 CVA Port P559
10 (left) Collection of Graeme Pole
10 (right) CPRA NS.3997
13 LAC PA-032428
16 (top) GP
16 (bottom) LAC PA-026427
19 (top) O.B. Buell, CPRA A.4227
19 (bottom) CPRA NS.9145
20 RMA P1740
21 GP
24 (left) CPRA A.75
24 (right) RRM A1993-76/647
25 W.M. Notman, NPA V1363
28 GMA NA 3026-13
31 GMA NA 1753-9
32 (top) O.B. Buell, GMA NA-4140-32
32 (bottom) W.M. Notman, NPA V2120
33 (top) W.M. Notman, detail from NPA V2120
33 (bottom) A.B. Thom, BCA F-03738

34 W.M. Notman, NPA V4771
35 RMA P1501
36 VPL 421
37 (top) GMA NA 1798-9
37 (bottom) GMA NA 2216-4
39 Nicholas Morant, RRM A1993-117/1112
42 O.B. Buell, LAC C-001402
43 (top) O.B. Buell, CPRA A.4212
43 (bottom) BCA B-06444
45 R.H. Trueman, WMCR V528/27-PA
46 GMA NA 4428-6
47 (top) W.M. Notman, NPA V3156
47 (bottom) VPL 851
48 E.C. Brooks, GMA NA 4432-4
49 R.H. Trueman, CVA 2-21
50 GMA NA 1459-2
52 RRM A2000-01/3057
56 (top) W.M. Notman, GMA NA 3740-26
56 (bottom) H.W. Gleason, Collection of Graeme Pole
57 (top) Bailey Brothers, VPL 19991
57 (bottom) Vaux family, WMCR-V653/NG-430
58 (top) A.B. Thom, NPA 93011026
58 (bottom) Collection of Graeme Pole
59 (top) GMA NA 4428-17
59 (bottom) Boorne and May, GMA NA 2115-2
60 (top) GMA NA 4428-4
60 (bottom) Norman Caple, CVA LGN 609

61 VPL 1758
62 A.B. Thom, NPA 93011015
63 VPL 829
64 Boorne and May, GMA NA 2216-6
65 Byron Harmon, BCA D-00183
66 GMA NA 2216-5
68 Byron Harmon, WMCR-V263/NA-1360
70 (top) O.B. Buell, GMA NA 4140-41
70 (bottom) O.B. Buell, GMA NA 4140-55
71 (top) A.B. Thom, RMA P1438
71 (bottom) W.M. Notman, NPA V1682
72 (top) RMA P1738
72 (bottom) BCA B-03845
73 (top) RRM A1997-02/2873
73 (bottom) R.H. Trueman, CVA 2-113
74 Byron Harmon, RRM A2000-01/3013
77 RRM A2000-02/3243
78 (top) Otto Klotz, BCA D-07155
78 (bottom) WMCR V650/2581-PD-19
79 RRM A2000-01/3098
80 (top) J.H.A. Chapman, BCA A-06672
80 (bottom) BCA A-09589
81 W.M. Notman, NPA View 1707
83 Mary Schäffer, GMA NA 345-30
84 Julia Henshaw, Collection of
    Graeme Pole
85 O.B. Buell, GMA NA 4140-30
88 (top) RRM A2000-02/3242

88 (mid) GMA NA 1263-36
88 (bottom) CPRA E6484-15
90 RRM A2000-01/3010
93 (top) RMA P2979
93 (bottom) RRM A2000-01/3031
94 RMA P1533
96 RRM A1995-04/1651
97 RRM A1995-04/1652
98 RRM
99 CPRA E-5706-34
101 Réjean Couture; reproduced
    with the permission of Natural
    Resources Canada 2008,
    courtesy of the Geological
    Survey of Canada
105 GP
107 GP
108 © Richard (BurghMan) Borkowski
110 RMA P1505
111 RMA P963
115 CVA Can P199
116 RRM A1993-25/264
118 GP
119 (top) Vaux family,
    WMCR V653 NG-674
119 (bottom) GP
121 (top) W.M. Notman, NPA V4755
121 (bottom) GP

Index